TREASURE OF
THE WESTERN WORLD

*Through the works of fifty great poets,
this volume presents a compact survey
of the poetry of the Western World from
ancient Greece to modern America.*

*In his selections, Milton Crane, editor of the
famous* FIFTY GREAT SHORT STORIES, *ranges
through Homer, Shakespeare, Keats,
Shelley, Heine, Baudelaire, Frost and
forty-three others most representative
of our poetic heritage.
Using large-scale selections, this book
is arranged to satisfy the requirements
of the serious student as well as
the lover of poetry.*

*Here is the enduring treasure
of the Western World,
the works of poets who have
captured and preserved the essential spirit
of their times while bringing
new and unique perceptions to all times.*

BANTAM POETRY

FIFTY GREAT POETS

Edited by Milton Crane

A NATIONAL GENERAL COMPANY

FIFTY GREAT POETS

A Bantam Classic / published July 1961
2nd printing ... December 1965   4th printing ... September 1968
3rd printing ..... October 1966   5th printing .... April 1970
Bantam edition published April 1972

The color photograph on the cover is by Morgan Kane.

Library of Congress Catalog Card Number: 65-28054

COPYRIGHTS AND ACKNOWLEDGMENTS

For permission to reprint all works in this volume by each of the following poets and translators, grateful acknowledgment is made to the holders of copyright, publishers or representatives named below and on pages v and vi which constitute an extension of this copyright page:

AUDEN, W. H.: *Something Is Bound to Happen* and *Petition.* From THE COLLECTED POETRY OF W. H. AUDEN © Copyright, 1934, by The Modern Library, Inc.; *Musee des Beaux Arts, In Memory of W. B. Yeats, September 1, 1939* and *The Unknown Citizen.* From THE COLLECTED POETRY OF W. H. AUDEN © Copyright, 1940, by W. H. Auden; *Who's Who* and *Oxford.* From THE COLLECTED POETRY OF W. H. AUDEN © Copyright, 1945, by W. H. Auden; *The Shield of Achilles.* From THE SHIELD OF ACHILLES by W. H. Auden © Copyright, 1952, by W. H. Auden; *Streams.* From THE SHIELD OF ACHILLES by W. H. Auden © Copyright, 1955, by W. H. Auden. Reprinted by permission of Random House, Inc. and by permission of Faber and Faber, Ltd., London.

BAUDELAIRE, CHARLES: *To The Reader, Voyage to Cythera, The Moon Offended* and *The Cat* (two poems). From POEMS OF BAUDELAIRE, translated by Roy Campbell. Copyrighted 1952 by Pantheon Books Inc. Reprinted by permission of Pantheon Books Inc. and the Narvill Press Ltd., London; *Litany to Satan* and *Don Juan in Hell.* Translated by J. E. Flecker. Copyright The Richards Press Ltd., London. Reprinted by permission of The Richards Press Ltd., London. *The Albatross* and *Correspondences.* Translated by Richard Wilbur. Copyright, 1955, by New Directions. Reprinted by permission of New Directions; *Giantess.* Reprinted by permission of Random House, Inc. From PERSON, PLACE AND THING by Karl Shapiro © Copyright, 1942, by Karl Shapiro; *Evening Harmony,* translated by Dorothy Martin, Copyright, 1955, by New Directions. Published in THE FLOWERS OF EVIL, edited by Jackson and Marthiel Mathews, and in SELECTED FLOWERS OF EVIL. Reprinted with permission of New Directions; *Invitation to the Voyage.* Translated by Richard Wilbur. From THINGS OF THIS WORLD, © 1956, by Richard Wilbur. Reprinted by permission of Harcourt, Brace and World, Inc.

CATULLUS: *Tell Me, Sparrow; My Woman Says; You Poor Catullus.* Translated by Gilbert Highet. From POETS IN A LANDSCAPE by Gilbert Highet, Copyright, 1957 by Gilbert Highet. Reprinted with permission of Alfred A. Knopf, Inc. and Hamish Hamilton, Ltd., London.

CHAUCER, GEOFFREY: *Prologue to The Wife of Bath's Tale.* From THE PORTABLE CHAUCER, selected, translated, and edited by Theodore Morrison. Copyright 1949 by Theodore Morrison. Reprinted by permission of The Viking Press, Inc.

DICKINSON, EMILY: *I Dwell in Possibility, After Great Pain, At Leisure Is the Soul*. From POEMS OF EMILY DICKINSON. Copyright, 1914, 1929, 1935, 1942 by Martha Dickinson Bianchi; Copyright, ©, 1957, by Mary L. Hampson. Reprinted by permission of Little, Brown and Company.

FROST, ROBERT: *The Tuft of Flowers, Mending Wall, The Road Not Taken, The Witch of Coös, Fire and Ice, On Looking Up by Chance at the Constellations, The Silken Tent, A Considerable Speck*, and *New Hampshire*. Extracts from THE COMPLETE POEMS OF ROBERT FROST. Copyright, 1930, 1949 by Holt, Rinehart & Winston, Inc. Reprinted by permission of the British publishers, Messrs. Jonathan Cape, Ltd., and the American publishers, Messrs. Holt, Rinehart & Winston, Inc.

HARDY, THOMAS: *Neutral Tones, Nature's Questioning, I Look into My Glass, The Last Chrysanthemum, The Darkling Thrush, The Ruined Maid, Let Me Enjoy, Former Beauties, Channel Firing, The Convergence of the Twain, The Schreckhorn, The Year's Awakening, The Oxen, During Wind and Rain, In Time of "The Breaking of the Nations," Afterward, Weathers, Epitaph, An Ancient to Ancients*. From COLLECTED POEMS OF THOMAS HARDY. ©, 1925, The Macmillan Company. Reprinted by permission of The Macmillan Company. Permission also granted by the Trustees of the Hardy Estate, Macmillan & Company, Ltd. and The Macmillan Company of Canada, Ltd.

HEINE, HEINRICH: *Tell Me Where Thy Lovely Love Is, The Mutilated Choir Boys, This Delightful Young Man*. From DIE HEIMKEHR. *I am the Princess Ilza*. From DIE HARZREISE, translated by Ezra Pound. Reprinted from PERSONAE, Copyright, 1926, by Ezra Pound, by permission of New Directions and by permission of Arthur V. Moore, Literary Agent for Ezra Pound; *The Azra*, translated by John Hay. Reprinted with the permission of Houghton Mifflin Company; The seven poems translated by Louis Untermeyer from HEINRICH HEINE: PARADOX AND POET, *The Poems* by Louis Untermeyer, Copyright, 1937, by Harcourt, Brace and World, Inc.

HOMER: *The Iliad, Book 1*. Translated by Richard Lattimore. Reprinted by permission of The University of Chicago Press, Copyright, 1951, by The University of Chicago and with the permission of Routledge and Kegan Paul Ltd. © Richard Lattimore.

HOPKINS, GERARD MANLEY: *The Windhover, Pied Beauty, Felix Randal, The Leaden Echo and the Golden Echo, I Wake and Feel the Fell of Dark, Duns Scotus's Oxford, Carrion Comfort, Hurrahing in Harvest, Spring, Spring and Fall, God's Grandeur*. From POEMS OF GERARD MANLEY HOPKINS. Third edition 1948. Reprinted by permission of Oxford University Press, Inc.

HORACE: *Invocation (Odes 1, 21)*. From INCLUDING HORACE by Louis Untermeyer, Copyright, 1919, by Harcourt, Brace and World, Inc.; renewed, 1947, by Louis Untermeyer. Reprinted by permission of the publishers. *Odes 1, 5*. Translated by Gilbert Highet. From POETS IN A LANDSCAPE by Gilbert Highet. Copyright 1957 by Gilbert Highet. Reprinted with permission of Alfred A. Knopf, Inc. and Hamish Hamilton, Ltd., London.

LORCA, FEDERICO GARCIA: *Preciosa and the Wind, The Unfaithful Married Woman, The Spanish Civil Guard, The Moon, the Moon, Walking Asleep*. From GYPSY BALLADS OF GARCIA LORCA. Translated by Rolfe Humphries. Copyright, 1953, by Rolfe Humphries and published by Indiana University Press. Reprinted with the permission of Indiana University Press. *Reyerta, The Death of Antonito el Camborio, Cordoba, The Guitar*. Translated by Roy Campbell. From GARCIA LORCA by Roy Campbell. Reprinted with permission of Bowes and Bowes Publishers Ltd., London

MOORE, MARIANNE: *Poetry, England, New York, To a Steamroller, Silence*. © 1935 by The Macmillan Company. From SELECTED POEMS by Marianne Moore; *Spenser's Ireland, What Are Years*. © 1941 by The Macmillan Company; *A Carriage from Sweden, The Mind is an Enchanting Thing*. © 1944 by The Macmillan Company; *Propriety*. © 1951 by The Macmillan Company. From COLLECTED POEMS by Marianne Moore, published by The Macmillan Company. Reprinted by permission of The Macmillan Company.

OVID: *(Amores II, 7), (Amores II, 8)*. Translated by Gilbert Highet. From POETS IN A LANDSCAPE by Gilbert Highet. Copyright, 1957, by Gilbert Highet. Reprinted by permission of Alfred A. Knopf, Inc., and Hamish Hamilton, Ltd., London.

RILKE, RAINER MARIA: *The Poet*. Translated by Selden Rodman. From 100 MODERN POEMS, published by The New American Library. Copyright, 1949, by Pellegrini & Cudahy. Reprinted by permission of the editor and translator, Selden Rodman; *Autumn*. Translated by Ernest Kroll. Copyright, 1959, Ernest Kroll. Reprinted with permission of Ernest Kroll; *Spanish Dancer, Grave Hour,*

Published simultaneously in the United States and Canada

Bantam Books are published by Bantam Books, Inc., a National General company. Its trade-mark, consisting of the words "Bantam Books" and the portrayal of a bantam, is registered in the United States Patent Office and in other countries. Marca Registrada. Bantam Books, Inc., 666 Fifth Avenue, New York, N.Y. 10019.

PRINTED IN THE UNITED STATES OF AMERICA

TO EVA AND FREDERICK LECHNER

pensate the reader for the omission of some of his old favorites.

I am deeply grateful for the wise counsel of my friends Joan and Stanley Bennett, Mark Van Doren, Ronald S. Crane, Thomas O. Mabbott, Ernest and Margaret Kroll, Edward W. Rosenheim, Jr., Henry Rago, and Grace Bechtold. Mark Van Doren's matchless *Anthology of World Poetry* guided me at a number of difficult points, as it has these many years. And I owe a special debt to Saul David for suggesting this book.

MILTON CRANE

The Song of Songs

WHICH IS SOLOMON'S

1

Let him kiss me with the kisses of his mouth: for thy love is better than wine.

Because of the savor of thy good ointments thy name is as ointment poured forth, therefore do the virgins love thee.

Draw me, we will run after thee: the king hath brought me into his chambers: we will be glad and rejoice in thee, we will remember thy love more than wine: the upright love thee.

I am black, but comely, O ye daughters of Jerusalem, as the tents of Kedar, as the curtains of Solomon.

Look not upon me, because I am black, because the sun hath looked upon me: my mother's children were angry with me; they made me the keeper of the vineyards; but mine own vineyard have I not kept.

Tell me, O thou whom my soul loveth, where thou feedest, where thou makest thy flock to rest at noon: for why should I be as one that turneth aside by the flocks of thy companions?

If thou know not, O thou fairest among women, go thy way forth by the footsteps of the flock, and feed thy kids beside the shepherds' tents.

I have compared thee, O my love, to a company of horses in Pharaoh's chariots.

Thy cheeks are comely with rows of jewels, thy neck with chains of gold.

We will make thee borders of gold with studs of silver.

While the king sitteth at his table, my spikenard sendeth forth the smell thereof.

A bundle of myrrh is my well-beloved unto me; he shall lie all night betwixt my breasts.

My beloved is unto me as a cluster of camphire in the vineyards of En-gedi.

Behold, thou art fair, my love; behold, thou art fair; thou hast doves' eyes.

Behold, thou art fair, my beloved, yea, pleasant: also our bed is green.

The beams of our house are cedar, and our rafters of fir.

2

I am the rose of Sharon, and the lily of the valleys.

As the lily among thorns, so is my love among the daughters.

As the apple tree among the trees of the wood, so is my beloved among the sons. I sat down under his shadow with great delight, and his fruit was sweet to my taste.

He brought me to the banqueting house, and his banner over me was love.

Stay me with flagons, comfort me with apples: for I am sick of love.

His left hand is under my head, and his right hand doth embrace me.

I charge you, O ye daughters of Jerusalem, by the roes, and by the hinds of the field, that ye stir not up, nor awake my love, till he please.

The voice of my beloved! behold, he cometh leaping upon the mountains, skipping upon the hills.

My beloved is like a roe or a young hart: behold, he standeth behind our wall, he looketh forth at the windows, shewing himself through the lattice.

My beloved spake, and said unto me, Rise up, my love, my fair one, and come away.

For, lo, the winter is past, the rain is over and gone;

The flowers appear on the earth; the time of the singing of birds is come, and the voice of the turtle is heard in our land;

The fig tree putteth forth her green figs, and the vines with the tender grape give a good smell. Arise, my love, my fair one, and come away.

O my dove, that art in the clefts of the rock, in the secret places of the stairs, let me see thy countenance, let me hear thy voice; for sweet is thy voice, and thy countenance is comely.

Take us the foxes, the little foxes, that spoil the vines: for our vines have tender grapes.

My beloved is mine, and I am his: he feedeth among the lilies.

Until the day break, and the shadows flee away, turn, my beloved, and be thou like a roe or a young hart upon the mountains of Bether.

3

By night on my bed I sought him whom my soul loveth: I sought him, but I found him not.

I will rise now, and go about the city in the streets, and in the broad ways I will seek him whom my soul loveth: I sought him, but I found him not.

The watchmen that go about the city found me; to whom I said, Saw ye him whom my soul loveth?

It was but a little that I passed from them, but I found him whom my soul loveth: I held him, and would not let him go, until I had brought him into my mother's house, and into the chamber of her that conceived me.

I charge you, O ye daughters of Jerusalem, by the roes, and by the hinds of the field, that ye stir not up, nor wake my love, till he please.

Who is this that cometh out of the wilderness like pillars of smoke, perfumed with myrrh and frankincense, with all powders of the merchant?

Behold his bed, which is Solomon's; three score valiant men are about it, of the valiant of Israel.

They all hold swords, being expert in war: every man hath his sword upon his thigh because of fear in the night.

King Solomon made himself a chariot of the wood of Lebanon.

He made the pillars thereof of silver, the bottom thereof of gold, the covering of it of purple, the midst thereof being paved with love, for the daughters of Jerusalem.

Go forth, O ye daughters of Zion, and behold king Solomon with the crown wherewith his mother crowned him in the day of his espousals, and in the day of the gladness of his heart.

4

Behold, thou art fair, my love; behold, thou art fair; thou hast doves' eyes within thy locks: thy hair is as a flock of goats, that appear from mount Gilead.

Thy teeth are like a flock of sheep that are even shorn, which came up from the washing; whereof every one bear twins, and none is barren among them.

Thy lips are like a thread of scarlet, and thy speech is comely: thy temples are like a piece of a pomegranate within thy locks.

Thy neck is like the tower of David builded for an armory, whereon there hang a thousand bucklers, all shields of mighty men.

Thy two breasts are like two young roes that are twins, which feed among the lilies.

Until the day break, and the shadows flee away, I will get me to the mountains of myrrh, and to the hill of frankincense.

Thou art all fair, my love; there is no spot in thee.

Come with me from Lebanon, my spouse, with me from Lebanon: look from the top of Amana, from the top of Shenir and Hermon, from the lions' dens, from the mountains of the leopards.

Thou hast ravished my heart, my sister, my spouse; thou hast ravished my heart with one of thine eyes, with one chain of thy neck.

How fair is thy love, my sister, my spouse! how much better is thy love than wine! and the smell of thine ointments than all spices!

Thy lips, O my spouse, drop as the honey-comb: honey and milk are under thy tongue; and the smell of thy garments is like the smell of Lebanon.

A garden inclosed is my sister, my spouse; a spring shut up, a fountain sealed.

Thy plants are an orchard of pomegranates, with pleasant fruits; camphire, with spikenard,

Spikenard and saffron; calamus and cinnamon, with all trees of frankincense; myrrh and aloes, with all the chief spices:

A fountain of gardens, a well of living waters, and streams from Lebanon.

Awake, O north wind; and come, thou south; blow upon my garden, that the spices thereof may flow out. Let my beloved come into his garden, and eat his pleasant fruits.

5

I am come into my garden, my sister, my spouse: I have gathered my myrrh with my spice; I have eaten my honey-comb with my honey; I have drunk my wine with my milk: eat, O friends; drink, yea, drink abundantly, O beloved.

I sleep, but my heart waketh: it is the voice of my beloved that knocketh, saying, Open to me, my sister, my love, my dove, my undefiled: for my head is filled with dew, and my locks with the drops of the night.

I have put off my coat; how shall I put it on? I have washed my feet; how shall I defile them?

My beloved put in his hand by the hole of the door, and my bowels were moved for him.

I rose up to open to my beloved; and my hands dropped with myrrh, and my fingers with sweet smelling myrrh, upon the handles of the lock.

I opened to my beloved; but my beloved had withdrawn himself, and was gone: my soul failed when he spake: I sought him, but I could not find him; I called him, but he gave me no answer.

The watchmen that went about the city found me, they smote me, they wounded me; the keepers of the walls took away my veil from me.

I charge you, O daughters of Jerusalem, if ye find my beloved, that ye tell him, that I am sick of love.

What is thy beloved more than another beloved, O thou fairest among women? what is thy beloved more than another beloved, that thou dost so charge us?

My beloved is white and ruddy, the chiefest among ten thousand.

His head is as the most fine gold, his locks are bushy, and black as a raven.

His eyes are as the eyes of doves by the rivers of waters, washed with milk, and fitly set.

His cheeks are as a bed of spices, as sweet flowers: his lips like lilies, dropping sweet smelling myrrh.

His hands are as gold rings set with the beryl: his belly is as bright ivory overlaid with sapphires.

His legs are as pillars of marble, set upon sockets of fine gold: his countenance is as Lebanon, excellent as the cedars.

His mouth is most sweet: yea, he is altogether lovely. This is my beloved, and this is my friend, O daughters of Jerusalem.

6

Whither is thy beloved gone, O thou fairest among women? whither is thy beloved turned aside? that we may seek him with thee?

My beloved is gone down into his garden, to the beds of spices, to feed in the gardens, and to gather lilies.

I am my beloved's, and my beloved is mine: he feedeth among the lilies.

Thou art beautiful, O my love, as Tirzah, comely as Jerusa-lem, terrible as an army with banners.

Turn away thine eyes from me, for they have overcome me: thy hair is as a flock of goats that appear from Gilead.

Thy teeth are as a flock of sheep which go up from the washing, whereof every one beareth twins, and there is not one barren among them.

As a piece of a pomegranate are thy temples within thy locks.

There are threescore queens, and fourscore concubines, and virgins without number.

My dove, my undefiled is but one; she is the only one of her mother, she is the choice one of her that bare her. The daughters saw her, and blessed her; yea, the queens and the concubines, and they praised her.

Who is she that looketh forth as the morning, fair as the moon, clear as the sun, and terrible as an army with banners?

I went down into the garden of nuts to see the fruits of the valley, and to see whether the vine flourished, and the pomegranates budded.

Or ever I was aware, my soul made me like the chariots of Ammi-nadib.

Return, return, O Shulamite; return, return, that we may look upon thee. What will ye see in the Shulamite? As it were the company of two armies.

7

How beautiful are thy feet with shoes. O prince's daughter! the joints of thy thighs are like jewels, the work of the hands of a cunning workman.

Thy navel is like a round goblet, which wanteth not liquor: thy belly is like an heap of wheat set about with lilies.

Thy two breasts are like two young roes that are twins.

Thy neck is as a tower of ivory; thine eyes like the fishpools in Heshbon, by the gate of Bathrabbim; thy nose is as the tower of Lebanon which looketh toward Damascus.

Thine head upon thee is like Carmel, and the hair of thine head like purple; the king is held in the galleries.

How fair and how pleasant art thou, O love, for delights!

This thy stature is like to a palm tree, and thy breasts to clusters of grapes.

I said, I will go up to the palm tree, I will take hold of the boughs thereof: now also thy breasts shall be as clusters of the vine, and the smell of thy nose like apples;

And the roof of thy mouth like the best wine for my beloved, that goeth down sweetly, causing the lips of those that are asleep to speak.

I am my beloved's, and his desire is toward me.

Come, my beloved, let us go forth into the field; let us lodge in the villages.

Let us get up early to the vineyards; let us see if the vine flourish, whether the tender grape appear, and the pomegranates bud forth: there will I give thee my loves.

The mandrakes give a smell, and at our gates are all manner of pleasant fruits, new and old, which I have laid up for thee, O my beloved.

8

O that thou wert as my brother, that sucked the breasts of my mother! when I should find thee without, I would kiss thee; yet, I should not be despised.

I would lead thee, and bring thee into my mother's house, who would instruct me: I would cause thee to drink of spiced wine of the juice of my pomegranate.

His left hand should be under my head, and his right hand should embrace me.

I charge you, O daughters of Jerusalem, that ye stir not up, nor awake my love, until he please.

Who is that cometh up from the wilderness, leaning upon her beloved? I raised thee up under the apple tree: there thy mother brought thee forth: there she brought thee forth that bare thee.

Set me as a seal upon thine heart, as a seal upon thine arm: for love is strong as death; jealousy is cruel as the grave: the coals thereof are coals of fire, which hath a most vehement flame.

Many waters cannot quench love, neither can the floods drown it: if a man would give all the substance of his house for love, it would utterly be contemned.

We have a little sister, and she hath no breasts: what shall we do for our sister in the day when she shall be spoken for?

If she be a wall, we will build upon her a palace of silver: and if she be a door, we will inclose her with boards of cedar.

I am a wall, and my breasts like towers: then was I in his eyes as one that found favor.

Solomon had a vineyard at Baalhamon; he let out the vineyard unto keepers; every one for the fruit thereof was to bring a thousand pieces of silver.

My vineyard, which is mine, is before me: thou, O Solomon, must have a thousand, and those that keep the fruit thereof two hundred.

Thou that dwellest in the gardens, the companions hearken to thy voice: cause me to hear it.

Make haste, my beloved, and be thou like to a roe or to a young hart upon the mountains of spices.

(King James Version)

Homer

fl. 850 B.C. or earlier

THE ILIAD, BOOK I

Sing, goddess, the anger of Peleus' son Achilleus
and its devastation, which put pains thousandfold upon the
Achaians,
hurled in their multitudes to the house of Hades strong souls
of heroes, but gave their bodies to be the delicate feasting
of dogs, of all birds, and the will of Zeus was accomplished
since that time when first there stood in division of conflict
Atreus' son the lord of men and brilliant Achilleus.

What god was it then set them together in bitter collision?
Zeus' son and Leto's, Apollo, who in anger at the king drove
the foul pestilence along the host, and the people perished,
since Atreus' son had dishonoured Chryses, priest of Apollo,
when he came beside the fast ships of the Achaians to ransom
back his daughter, carrying gifts beyond count and holding
in his hands wound on a staff of gold the ribbons of Apollo
who strikes from afar, and supplicated all the Achaians,
but above all Atreus' two sons, the marshals of the people:
'Sons of Atreus and you other strong-greaved Achaians,
to you may the gods grant who have their homes on Olympos
Priam's city to be plundered and a fair homecoming thereafter,
but may you give me back my own daughter and take the
ransom,
giving honour to Zeus' son who strikes from afar, Apollo.'

Then all the rest of the Achaians cried out in favour
that the priest be respected and the shining ransom be taken;
yet this pleased not the heart of Atreus' son Agamemnon,
but harshly he drove him away with a strong order upon him:
'Never let me find you again, old sir, near our hollow
ships, neither lingering now nor coming again hereafter,
for fear your staff and the god's ribbons help you no longer.
The girl I will not give back; sooner will old age come upon her
in my own house, in Argos, far from her own land, going
up and down by the loom and being in my bed as my
companion.
So go now, do not make me angry; so you will be safer.'

So he spoke, and the old man in terror obeyed him
and went silently away beside the murmuring sea beach.
Over and over the old man prayed as he walked in solitude
to King Apollo, whom Leto of the lovely hair bore: 'Hear me,
lord of the silver bow who set your power about Chryse

and Killa the sacrosanct, who are lord in strength over
    Tenedos,
Smintheus, if ever it pleased your heart that I built your
    temple,
if ever it pleased you that I burned all the rich thigh pieces
of bulls, of goats, then bring to pass this wish I pray for:
let your arrows make the Danaans pay for my tears shed.'
    So he spoke in prayer, and Phoibos Apollo heard him,
and strode down along the pinnacles of Olympos, angered
in his heart, carrying across his shoulders the bow and the
    hooded
quiver; and the shafts clashed on the shoulders of the god
    walking
angrily. He came as night comes down and knelt then
apart and opposite the ships and let go an arrow.
Terrible was the clash that rose from the bow of silver.
First he went after the mules and the circling hounds, then let
    go
a tearing arrow against the men themselves and struck them.
The corpse fires burned everywhere and did not stop burning.
    Nine days up and down the host ranged the god's arrows,
but on the tenth Achilleus called the people to assembly;
a thing put into his mind by the goddess of the white arms,
    Hera,
who had pity upon the Danaans when she saw them dying.
Now when they were all assembled in one place together,
Achilleus of the swift feet stood up among them and spoke
    forth:
'Son of Atreus, I believe now that straggling backwards
we must make our way home if we can even escape death,
if fighting now must crush the Achaians and the plague
    likewise.
No, come, let us ask some holy man, some prophet,
even an interpreter of dreams, since a dream also
comes from Zeus, who can tell why Phoibos Apollo is so angry,
if for the sake of some vow, some hecatomb he blames us,
if given the fragrant smoke of lambs, of he goats, somehow
he can be made willing to beat the bane aside from us.'
    He spoke thus and sat down again, and among them stood up
Kalchas, Thestor's son, far the best of the bird interpreters,
who knew all things that were, the things to come and the
    things past,
who guided into the land of Ilion the ships of the Achaians
through that seercraft of his own that Phoibos Apollo gave
    him.
He in kind intention toward all stood forth and addressed
    them:
'You have bidden me, Achilleus beloved of Zeus, to explain to
you this anger of Apollo the lord who strikes from afar. Then
I will speak; yet make me a promise and swear before me
readily by word and work of your hands to defend me,
since I believe I shall make a man angry who holds great
    kingship
over the men of Argos, and all the Achaians obey him.

For a king when he is angry with a man beneath him is too
    strong,
and suppose even for the day itself he swallow down his anger,
he still keeps bitterness that remains until its fulfilment
deep in his chest. Speak forth then, tell me if you will protect
    me.'
    Then in answer again spoke Achilleus of the swift feet;
'Speak, interpreting whatever you know, and fear nothing.
In the name of Apollo beloved of Zeus to whom you, Kalchas,
make your prayers when you interpret the gods' will to the
    Danaans,
no man so long as I am alive above earth and see daylight
shall lay the weight of his hands on you beside the hollow
    ships,
not one of all the Danaans, even if you mean Agamemnon,
who now claims to be far the greatest of all the Achaians.'
    At this the blameless seer took courage again and spoke
    forth:
'No, it is not for the sake of some vow or hecatomb he blames
    us,
but for the sake of his priest whom Agamemnon dishonoured
and would not give him back his daughter nor accept the
    ransom.
Therefore the archer sent griefs against us and will send them
still, nor sooner thrust back the shameful plague from the
    Danaans
until we give the glancing-eyed girl back to her father
without price, without ransom, and lead also a blessed
    hecatomb
to Chryse; thus we might propitiate and persuade him.'
    He spoke thus and sat down again, and among them stood up
Atreus' son the hero wide-ruling Agamemnon
raging, the heart within filled black to the brim with anger
from beneath, but his two eyes showed like fire in their blazing.
First of all he eyed Kalchas bitterly and spoke to him:
'Seer of evil: never yet have you told me a good thing.
Always the evil things are dear to your heart to prophesy,
but nothing excellent have you said nor ever accomplished.
Now once more you make divination to the Danaans, argue
forth your reason why he who strikes from afar afflicts them,
because I for the sake of the girl Chryseis would not take
the shining ransom; and indeed I wish greatly to have her
in my own house; since I like her better than Klytaimnestra
my own wife, for in truth she is no way inferior,
neither in build nor stature nor wit, nor in accomplishment.
Still I am willing to give her back, if such is the best way.
I myself desire that my people be safe, not perish.
Find me then some prize that shall be my own, lest I only
among the Argives go without, since that were unfitting;
you are all witnesses to this thing, that my prize goes
    elsewhere.'
    Then in answer again spoke brilliant swift-footed Achilleus:
'Son of Atreus, most lordly, greediest for gain of all men,
how shall the great-hearted Achaians give you a prize now?

There is no great store of things lying about I know of.
But what we took from the cities by storm has been
    distributed;
it is unbecoming for the people to call back things once given.
No, for the present give the girl back to the god; we Achaians
thrice and four times over will repay you, if ever Zeus gives
into our hands the strong-walled citadel of Troy to be
    plundered.'
    Then in answer again spoke powerful Agamemnon:
'Not that way, good fighter though you be, godlike Achilleus,
strive to cheat, for you will not deceive, you will not persuade
    me.
What do you want? To keep your own prize and have me sit
    here
lacking one? Are you ordering me to give this girl back?
Either the great-hearted Achaians shall give me a new prize
chosen according to my desire to atone for the girl lost,
or else if they will not give me one I myself shall take her,
your own prize, or that of Aias, or that of Odysseus,
going myself in person; and he whom I visit will be bitter.
Still, these are things we shall deliberate again hereafter.
Come, now, we must haul a black ship down to the bright sea,
and assemble rowers enough for it, and put on board it
the hecatomb, and the girl herself, Chryseis of the fair cheeks,
and let there be one responsible man in charge of her,
either Aias or Idomeneus or brilliant Odysseus,
or you yourself, son of Peleus, most terrifying of all men,
to reconcile by accomplishing sacrifice the archer.'
    Then looking darkly at him Achilleus of the swift feet
    spoke:
'O wrapped in shamelessness, with your mind forever on profit,
how shall any one of the Achaians readily obey you
either to go on a journey or to fight men strongly in battle?
I for my part did not come here for the sake of the Trojan
spearmen to fight against them, since to me they have done
    nothing.
Never yet have they driven away my cattle or my horses,
never in Phthia where the soil is rich and men grow great
    did they
spoil my harvest, since indeed there is much that lies between
    us,
the shadowy mountains and the echoing sea; but for your
    sake,
o great shamelessness, we followed, to do you favour,
you with the dog's eyes, to win your honour and Menelaos'
from the Trojans. You forget all this or else you care nothing.
And now my prize you threaten in person to strip from me,
for whom I laboured much, the gift of the sons of the
    Achaians.
Never, when the Achaians sack some well-founded citadel
of the Trojans, do I have a prize that is equal to your prize.
Always the greater part of the painful fighting is the work of
my hands; but when the time comes to distribute the booty
yours is far the greater reward, and I with some small thing

yet dear to me go back to my ships when I am weary with
fighting.
Now I am returning to Phthia, since it is much better
to go home again with my curved ships, and I am minded no
longer
to stay here dishonoured and pile up your wealth and your
luxury.'
    Then answered him in turn the lord of men Agamemnon:
'Run away by all means if your heart drives you. I will not
entreat you to stay here for my sake. There are others with me
who will do me honour, and above all Zeus of the counsels.
To me you are the most hateful of all the kings whom the
gods love.
Forever quarrelling is dear to your heart, and wars and
battles;
and if you are very strong indeed, that is a god's gift.
Go home then with your own ships and your own companions,
be king over the Myrmidons. I care nothing about you.
I take no account of your anger. But here is my threat to you.
Even as Phoibos Apollo is taking away my Chryseis.
I shall convey her back in my own ship, with my own
followers; but I shall take the fair-cheeked Briseis,
your prize, I myself going to your shelter, that you may learn
well
how much greater I am than you, and another man may shrink
back
from likening himself to me and contending against me.'
    So he spoke. And the anger came on Peleus' son, and within
his shaggy breast the heart was divided two ways, pondering
whether to draw from beside his thigh the sharp sword,
driving
away all those who stood between and kill the son of Atreus,
or else to check the spleen within and keep down his anger.
Now as he weighed in mind and spirit these two courses
and was drawing from its scabbard the great sword, Athene
descended
from the sky. For Hera the goddess of the white arms sent her,
who loved both men equally in her heart and cared for them.
The goddess standing behind Peleus' son caught him by the
fair hair,
appearing to him only, for no man of the others saw her.
Achilleus in amazement turned about, and straightway
knew Pallas Athene and the terrible eyes shining.
He uttered winged words and addressed her: 'Why have you
come now,
o child of Zeus of the aegis, once more? Is it that you may see
the outrageousness of the son of Atreus Agamemnon?
Yet will I tell you this thing, and I think it shall be
accomplished.
By such acts of arrogance he may even lose his own life.'
    Then in answer the goddess grey-eyed Athene spoke to him:
'I have come down to stay your anger—but will you obey
me?—
from the sky; and the goddess of the white arms Hera sent me,
who loves both of you equally in her heart and cares for you.

Come then, do not take your sword in your hand, keep clear of
    fighting,
though indeed with words you may abuse him, and it will be
    that way.
And this also will I tell you and it will be a thing accomplished.
Some day three times over such shining gifts shall be given
    you
by reason of this outrage. Hold your hand then, and obey us.'
    Then in answer again spoke Achilleus of the swift feet:
'Goddess, it is necessary that I obey the word of you two,
angry though I am in my heart. So it will be better.
If any man obeys the gods, they listen to him also.'
    He spoke, and laid his heavy hand on the silver sword hilt
and thrust the great blade back into the scabbard nor
    disobeyed
the word of Athene. And she went back again to Olympos
to the house of Zeus of the aegis with the other divinities.
    But Peleus' son once again in words of derision
spoke to Atreides, and did not yet let go of his anger:
'You wine sack, with a dog's eyes, with a deer's heart. Never
once have you taken courage in your heart to arm with your
    people
for battle, or go into ambuscade with the best of the Achaians.
No, for in such things you see death. Far better to your mind
is it, all along the widespread host of the Achaians
to take away the gifts of any man who speaks up against you.
King who feed on your people, since you rule nonentities;
otherwise, son of Atreus, this were your last outrage.
But I will tell you this and swear a great oath upon it:
in the name of this sceptre, which never again will bear leaf
    nor
branch, now that it has left behind the cut stump in the
    mountains,
nor shall it ever blossom again, since the bronze blade stripped
bark and leafage, and now at last the sons of the Achaians
carry it in their hands in state when they administer
the justice of Zeus. And this shall be a great oath before you:
some day longing for Achilleus will come to the sons of the
    Achaians,
all of them. Then stricken at heart though you be, you will be
    able
to do nothing, when in their numbers before man-slaughtering
    Hektor
they drop and die. And then you will eat out the heart within
    you
in sorrow, that you did no honour to the best of the Achaians.'
    Thus spoke Peleus' son and dashed to the ground the sceptre
studded with golden nails, and sat down again. But Atreides
raged still on the other side, and between them Nestor
the fair-spoken rose up, the lucid speaker of Pylos,
from whose lips the streams of words ran sweeter than honey.
In his time two generations of mortal men had perished,
those who had grown up with him and they who had been
    born to

these in sacred Pylos, and he was king in the third age.
He in kind intention toward both stood forth and addressed
    them:
'Oh, for shame. Great sorrow comes on the land of Achaia.
Now might Priam and the sons of Priam in truth be happy,
and all the rest of the Trojans be visited in their hearts with
    gladness,
were they to hear all this wherein you two are quarrelling,
you, who surpass all Danaans in council, in fighting.
Yet be persuaded. Both of you are younger than I am.
Yes, and in my time I have dealt with better men than
you are, and never once did they disregard me. Never
yet have I seen nor shall see again such men as these were,
men like Peirithoös, and Dryas, shepherd of the people,
Kaineus and Exadios, godlike Polyphemos,
or Theseus, Aigeus' son, in the likeness of the immortals.
These were the strongest generation of earth-born mortals,
the strongest, and they fought against the strongest, the
    beast men
living within the mountains, and terribly they destroyed them.
I was of the company of these men, coming from Pylos,
a long way from a distant land, since they had summoned me.
And I fought single-handed, yet against such men no one
of the mortals now alive upon earth could do battle. And also
these listened to the counsels I gave and heeded my bidding.
Do you also obey, since to be persuaded is better.
You, great man that you are, yet do not take the girl away
but let her be, a prize as the sons of the Achaians gave her
first. Nor, son of Peleus, think to match your strength with
the king, since never equal with the rest is the portion of
    honour
of the sceptred king to whom Zeus gives magnificence. Even
though you are the stronger man, and the mother who bore
    you was immortal,
yet is this man greater who is lord over more than you rule.
Son of Atreus, give up your anger; even I entreat you
to give over your bitterness against Achilleus, he who
stands as a great bulwark of battle over all the Achaians.'
    Then in answer again spoke powerful Agamemnon:
'Yes, old sir, all this you have said is fair and orderly.
Yet here is a man who wishes to be above all others,
who wishes to hold power over all, and to be lord of
all, and give them their orders, yet I think one will not obey
    him.
And if the everlasting gods have made him a spearman,
yet they have not given him the right to speak abusively.'
    Then looking at him darkly brilliant Achilleus answered
    him:
'So must I be called of no account and a coward
if I must carry out every order you may happen to give me.
Tell other men to do these things, but give me no more
commands, since I for my part have no intention to obey you.
And put away in your thoughts this other thing I tell you.
With my hands I will not fight for the girl's sake, neither

with you nor any other man, since you take her away who
gave her.
But of all the other things that are mine beside my fast black
ship, you shall take nothing away against my pleasure.
Come, then, only try it, that these others may see also;
instantly your own black blood will stain my spearpoint.'
    So these two after battling in words of contention
stood up, and broke the assembly beside the ships of the
    Achaians.
Peleus' son went back to his balanced ships and his shelter
with Patroklos, Menoitios' son, and his own companions.
But the son of Atreus drew a fast ship down to the water
and allotted into it twenty rowers and put on board it
the hecatomb for the god and Chryseis of the fair cheeks
leading her by the hand. And in charge went crafty Odysseus.
    These then putting out went over the ways of the water
while Atreus' son told his people to wash off their defilement.
And they washed it away and threw the washings into the
    salt sea.
Then they accomplished perfect hecatombs to Apollo,
of bulls and goats along the beach of the barren salt sea.
The savour of the burning swept in circles up to the bright
    sky.
    Thus these were busy about the army. But Agamemnon
did not give up his anger and the first threat he made to
    Achilleus,
but to Talthybios he gave his orders and Eurybates
who were heralds and hard-working henchmen to him: 'Go
    now
to the shelter of Peleus' son Achilleus, to bring back
Briseis of the fair cheeks leading her by the hand. And if he
will not give her, I must come in person to take her
with many men behind me, and it will be the worse for him.'
    He spoke and sent them forth with this strong order upon
    them.
They went against their will beside the beach of the barren
salt sea, and came to the shelters and the ships of the
    Myrmidons.
The man himself they found beside his shelter and his black
    ship
sitting. And Achilleus took no joy at all when he saw them.
These two terrified and in awe of the king stood waiting
quietly, and did not speak a word at all nor question him.
But he knew the whole matter in his own heart, and spoke
    first:
'Welcome, heralds, messengers of Zeus and of mortals.
Draw near. You are not to blame in my sight, but Agamemnon
who sent the two of you here for the sake of the girl Briseis.
Go then, illustrious Patroklos, and bring the girl forth
and give her to these to be taken away. Yet let them be
    witnesses
in the sight of the blessed gods, in the sight of mortal
men, and of this cruel king, if ever hereafter
there shall be need of me to beat back the shameful destruction
from the rest. For surely in ruinous heart he makes sacrifice

and has not wit enough to look behind and before him
that the Achaians fighting beside their ships shall not perish.'
    So he spoke, and Patroklos obeyed his beloved companion.
He led forth from the hut Briseis of the fair cheeks and gave
    her
to be taken away; and they walked back beside the ships of
    the Achaians,
and the woman all unwilling went with them still. But
    Achilleus
weeping went and sat in sorrow apart from his companions
beside the beach of the grey sea looking out on the infinite
    water.
Many times stretching forth his hands he called on his mother:
'Since, my mother, you bore me to be a man with a short life,
therefore Zeus of the loud thunder on Olympos should grant
    me
honour at least. But now he has given me not even a little.
Now the son of Atreus, powerful Agamemnon,
has dishonoured me, since he has taken away my prize and
    keeps it.'
    So he spoke in tears and the lady his mother heard him
as she sat in the depths of the sea at the side of her aged
    father,
and lightly she emerged like a mist from the grey water.
She came and sat beside him as he wept, and stroked him
with her hand and called him by name and spoke to him:
    'Why then,
child, do you lament? What sorrow has come to your heart
    now?
Tell me, do not hide it in your mind, and thus we shall both
    know.'
    Sighing heavily Achilleus of the swift feet answered her:
'You know; since you know why must I tell you all this?
We went against Thebe, the sacred city of Eëtion,
and the city we sacked, and carried everything back to this
    place,
and the sons of the Achaians made a fair distribution
and for Atreus' son they chose out Chryseis of the fair cheeks.
Then Chryses, priest of him who strikes from afar, Apollo,
came beside the fast ships of the bronze-armoured Achaians
    to ransom
back his daughter, carrying gifts beyond count and holding
in his hands wound on a staff of gold the ribbons of Apollo
who strikes from afar, and supplicated all the Achaians,
but above all Atreus' two sons, the marshals of the people.
Then all the rest of the Achaians cried out in favour
that the priest be respected and the shining ransom be taken;
yet this pleased not the heart of Atreus' son Agamemnon,
but harshly he sent him away with a strong order upon him.
The old man went back again in anger, but Apollo
listened to his prayer, since he was very dear to him, and let go
the wicked arrow against the Argives. And now the people
were dying one after another while the god's shafts ranged
everywhere along the wide host of the Achaians, till the seer
knowing well the truth interpreted the designs of the archer.

It was I first of all urged then the god's appeasement;
and the anger took hold of Atreus' son, and in speed standing
he uttered his threat against me, and now it is a thing
    accomplished.
For the girl the glancing-eyed Achaians are taking to Chryse
in a fast ship, also carrying to the king presents. But even
now the heralds went away from my shelter leading
Briseus' daughter, whom the sons of the Achaians gave me.
You then, if you have power to, protect your own son, going
to Olympos and supplicating Zeus, if ever before now
either by word you comforted Zeus' heart or by action.
Since it is many times in my father's halls I have heard you
making claims, when you said you only among the immortals
beat aside shameful destruction from Kronos' son the dark-
    misted,
that time when all the other Olympians sought to bind him,
Hera and Poseidon and Pallas Athene. Then you,
goddess, went and set him free from his shackles, summoning
in speed the creature of the hundred hands to tall Olympos,
that creature the gods name Briareus, but all men
Aigaios' son, but he is far greater in strength than his father.
He rejoicing in the glory of it sat down by Kronion,
and the rest of the blessed gods were frightened and gave up
    binding him.
Sit beside him and take his knees and remind him of these
    things
now, if perhaps he might be willing to help the Trojans,
and pin the Achaians back against the ships and the water,
dying, so that thus they may all have profit of their own king,
that Atreus' son wide-ruling Agamemnon may recognize
his madness, that he did no honour to the best of the Achaians.'

    Thetis answered him then letting the tears fall: 'Ah me,
my child. Your birth was bitterness. Why did I raise you?
If only you could sit by your ships untroubled, not weeping,
since indeed your lifetime is to be short, of no length.
Now it has befallen that your life must be brief and bitter
beyond all men's. To a bad destiny I bore you in my chambers.
But I will go to cloud-dark Olympos and ask this
thing of Zeus who delights in the thunder. Perhaps he will
    do it.
Do you therefore continuing to sit by your swift ships
be angry at the Achaians and stay away from all fighting.
For Zeus went to the blameless Aithiopians at the Ocean
yesterday to feast, and the rest of the gods went with him.
On the twelfth day he will be coming back to Olympos,
and then I will go for your sake to the house of Zeus, bronze-
    founded,
and take him by the knees and I think I can persuade him.'

    So speaking she went away from that place and left him
sorrowing in his heart for the sake of the fair-girdled woman
whom they were taking by force against his will. But Odysseus
meanwhile drew near to Chryse conveying the sacred
    hecatomb.
These when they were inside the many-hollowed harbour

took down and gathered together the sails and stowed them in
    the black ship,
let down mast by the forestays, and settled it into the mast
    crutch
easily, and rowed her in with oars to the mooring.
They threw over the anchor stones and made fast the stern
    cables
and themselves stepped out on to the break of the sea beach,
and led forth the hecatomb to the archer Apollo.
and Chryseis herself stepped forth from the sea-going vessel.
Odysseus of the many designs guided her to the altar
and left her in her father's arms and spoke a word to him:
'Chryses, I was sent here by the lord of men Agamemnon
to lead back your daughter and accomplish a sacred hecatomb
to Apollo on behalf of the Danaans, that we may propitiate
the lord who has heaped unhappiness and tears on the
    Argives.'
   He spoke, and left her in his arms. And he received gladly
his beloved child. And the men arranged the sacred hecatomb
for the god in orderly fashion around the strong-founded altar.
Next they washed their hands and took up the scattering
    barley.
Standing among them with lifted arms Chryses prayed in a
    great voice:
'Hear me, lord of the silver bow, who set your power about
Chryse and Killa the sacrosanct, who are lord in strength over
Tenedos; if once before you listened to my prayers
and did me honour and smote strongly the host of the
    Achaians,
so one more time bring to pass the wish that I pray for.
Beat aside at last the shameful plague from the Danaans.'
   So he spoke in prayer, and Phoibos Apollo heard him.
And when all had made prayer and flung down the scattering
    barley
first they drew back the victims' heads and slaughtered them
    and skinned them,
and cut away the meat from the thighs and wrapped them
    in fat,
making a double fold, and laid shreds of flesh upon them.
The old man burned these on a cleft stick and poured the
    gleaming
wine over, while the young men with forks in their hands
    stood about him.
But when they had burned the thigh pieces and tasted the
    vitals,
they cut all the remainder into pieces and spitted them
and roasted all carefully and took off the pieces.
Then after they had finished the work and got the feast
    ready
they feasted, nor was any man's hunger denied a fair portion.
But when they had put away their desire for eating and
    drinking,
the young men filled the mixing bowls with pure wine, passing
a portion to all, when they had offered drink in the goblets.

All day long they propitiated the god with singing,
chanting a splendid hymn to Apollo, these young Achaians,
singing to the one who works from afar, who listened in
    gladness.
  Afterwards when the sun went down and darkness came
    onward
they lay down and slept beside the ship's stern cables.
But when the young Dawn showed again with her rosy fingers,
they put forth to sea toward the wide camp of the Achaians.
And Apollo who works from afar sent them a favouring stern
    wind.
They set up the mast again and spread on it the white sails,
and the wind blew into the middle of the sail, and at the
    cutwater
a blue wave rose and sang strongly as the ship went onward.
She ran swiftly cutting across the swell her pathway.
But when they had come back to the wide camp of the
    Achaians
they hauled the black ship up on the mainland, high up
on the sand, and underneath her they fixed the long props.
Afterwards they scattered to their own ships and their
    shelters.
  But that other still sat in anger beside his swift ships,
Peleus' son divinely born, Achilleus of the swift feet.
Never now would he go to assemblies where men win glory,
never more into battle, but continued to waste his heart out
sitting there, though he longed always for the clamour and
    fighting.
  But when the twelfth dawn after this day appeared, the
    gods who
live forever came back to Olympos all in a body
and Zeus led them; nor did Thetis forget the entreaties
of her son, but she emerged from the sea's waves early
in the morning and went up to the tall sky and Olympos.
She found Kronos' broad-browed son apart from the others
sitting upon the highest peak of rugged Olympos.
She came and sat beside him with her left hand embracing
his knees, but took him underneath the chin with her right
    hand
and spoke in supplication to lord Zeus son of Kronos:
'Father Zeus, if ever before in word or action
I did you favour among the immortals, now grant what I ask
    for.
Now give honour to my son short-lived beyond all other
mortals. Since even now the lord of men Agamemnon
dishonours him, who has taken away his prize and keeps it.
Zeus of the counsels, lord of Olympos, now do him honour.
So long put strength into the Trojans, until the Achaians
give my son his rights, and his honour is increased among
    them.'
  She spoke thus. But Zeus who gathers the clouds made no
    answer
but sat in silence a long time. And Thetis, as she had taken
his knees, clung fast to them and urged once more her
    question:

'Bend your head and promise me to accomplish this thing,
or else refuse it, you have nothing to fear, that I may know
by how much I am the most dishonoured of all gods.'
    Deeply disturbed Zeus who gathers the clouds answered
        her:
'This is a disastrous matter when you set me in conflict
with Hera, and she troubles me with recriminations.
Since even as things are, forever among the immortals
she is at me and speaks of how I help the Trojans in battle.
Even so, go back again now, go away, for fear she
see us. I will look to these things that they be accomplished.
See then, I will bend my head that you may believe me.
For this among the immortal gods is the mightiest witness
I can give, and nothing I do shall be vain nor revocable
nor a thing unfulfilled when I bend my head in assent to it.'
    He spoke, the son of Kronos, and nodded his head with the
        dark brows,
and the immortally anointed hair of the great god
swept from his divine head, and all Olympos was shaken.
    So these two who had made their plans separated, and
        Thetis
leapt down again from shining Olympos into the sea's depth,
but Zeus went back to his own house, and all the gods rose up
from their chairs to greet the coming of their father, not one
        had courage
to keep his place as the father advanced, but stood up to greet
        him.
Thus he took his place on the throne; yet Hera was not
        ignorant, having seen how he had been plotting counsels
with Thetis the silver-footed, the daughter of the sea's ancient,
and at once she spoke revilingly to Zeus son of Kronos:
'Treacherous one, what god has been plotting counsels with
        you?
Always it is dear to your heart in my absence to think of
secret things and decide upon them. Never have you patience
frankly to speak forth to me the thing that you purpose.'
    Then to her the father of gods and men made answer:
'Hera, do not go on hoping that you will hear all my
thoughts, since these will be too hard for you, though you are
        my wife.
Any thought that it is right for you to listen to, no one
neither man nor any immortal shall hear it before you.
But anything that apart from the rest of the gods I wish to
plan, do not always question each detail nor probe me.'
    Then the goddess the ox-eyed lady Hera answered:
'Majesty, son of Kronos, what sort of thing have you spoken?
Truly too much in time past I have not questioned nor probed
        you,
but you are entirely free to think out whatever pleases you.
Now, though, I am terribly afraid you were won over
by Thetis the silver-footed, the daughter of the sea's ancient.
For early in the morning she sat beside you and took your
knees, and I think you bowed your head in assent to do honour
to Achilleus, and to destroy many beside the ships of the
        Achaians.'

Then in return Zeus who gathers the clouds made answer:
'Dear lady, I never escape you, you are always full of
    suspicion.
Yet thus you can accomplish nothing surely, but be more
distant from my heart than ever, and it will be the worse for
    you.
If what you say is true, then that is the way I wish it.
But go then, sit down in silence, and do as I tell you,
for fear all the gods, as many as are on Olympos, can do
    nothing
if I come close and lay my unconquerable hands upon you.'
    He spoke, and the goddess the ox-eyed lady Hera was
        frightened
and went and sat down in silence wrenching her heart to
    obedience,
and all the Uranian gods in the house of Zeus were troubled.
Hephaistos the renowned smith rose up to speak among them,
to bring comfort to his beloved mother, Hera of the white
    arms:
'This will be a disastrous matter and not endurable
if you two are to quarrel thus for the sake of mortals
and bring brawling among the gods. There will be no pleasure
in the stately feast at all, since vile things will be uppermost.
And I entreat my mother, though she herself understands it,
to be ingratiating toward our father Zeus, that no longer
our father may scold her and break up the quiet of our
    feasting.
For if the Olympian who handles the lightning should be
    minded
to hurl us out of our places, he is far too strong for any.
Do you therefore approach him again with words made gentle,
and at once the Olympian will be gracious again to us.'
    He spoke, and springing to his feet put a two-handled
        goblet
into his mother's hands and spoke again to her once more:
'Have patience, my mother, and endure it, though you be
    saddened,
for fear that, dear as you are, I see you before my own eyes
struck down, and then sorry though I be I shall not be able
to do anything. It is too hard to fight against the Olympian.
There was a time once before now I was minded to help you,
and he caught me by the foot and threw me from the magic
    threshold,
and all day long I dropped helpless, and about sunset
I landed in Lemnos, and there was not much life left in me.
After that fall it was the Sintian men who took care of me.'
    He spoke, and the goddess of the white arms Hera smiled
        at him,
and smiling she accepted the goblet out of her son's hand.
Thereafter beginning from the left he poured drinks for
    the other
gods, dipping up from the mixing bowl the sweet nectar.
But among the blessed immortals uncontrollable laughter
went up as they saw Hephaistos bustling about the palace.
    Thus thereafter the whole day long until the sun went under

they feasted, nor was anyone's hunger denied a fair portion,
nor denied the beautifully wrought lyre in the hands of Apollo
nor the antiphonal sweet sound of the Muses singing.
  Afterwards when the light of the flaming sun went under
they went away each one to sleep in his home where
for each one the far-renowned strong-handed Hephaistos
had built a house by means of his craftmanship and cunning.
Zeus the Olympian and lord of the lightning went to
his own bed, where always he lay when sweet sleep came on
  him.
Going up to the bed he slept and Hera of the gold throne
  beside him.

translated by RICHMOND LATTIMORE

Catullus

CAIUS VALERIUS CATULLUS—87-57 B.C.

MY SWEETEST LESBIA

My sweetest Lesbia, let us live and love,
And though the sager sort our deeds reprove,
Let us not weigh them. Heaven's great lamps do dive
Into their west, and straight again revive,
But, soon as once set is our little light,
Then must we sleep one ever-during night.

If all would lead their lives in love like me,
Then bloody swords and armor should not be;
No drum nor trumpet peaceful sleeps should move,
Unless alarm came from the camp of Love:
But fools do live and waste their little light,
And seek with pain their ever-during night.

When timely death my life and fortune ends,
Let not my hearse be vext with mourning friends,
But let all lovers rich in triumph come
And with sweet pastimes grace my happy tomb:
And, Lesbia, close up thou my little light,
And crown with love my ever-during night.

translated by THOMAS CAMPION

KISS ME, SWEET

Kiss me, sweet: the wary lover
Can your favors keep, and cover,
When the common courting jay
All your bounties will betray.
Kiss again! no creature comes;
Kiss, and score up wealthy sums
On my lips, thus hardly sundered,
While you breathe. First give a hundred,
Then a thousand, then another
Hundred, then unto the other
Add a thousand, and so more;
Till you equal with the store
All the grass that Romney yields,
Or the sands in Chelsea fields,
Or the drops in silver Thames,
Or the stars that gild his streams
In the silent summer-nights,
When youths ply their stolen delights;
That the curious may not know

How to tell 'em as they flow,
And the envious when they find
What their number is, be pined.

translated by BEN JONSON

PITY! MOURN IN PLAINTIVE TONE

Pity! mourn in plaintive tone
The lovely starling dead and gone!
  Pity mourns in plaintive tone
The lovely starling dead and gone.
Weep, ye Loves! and Venus! weep
The lovely starling fallen asleep!
Venus sees with tearful eyes—
In her lap the starling lies!
While the Loves all in a ring
Softly stroke the stiffened wing.

translated by SAMUEL TAYLOR COLERIDGE

LESBIA FOREVER ON ME RAILS

Lesbia forever on me rails.
To talk of me she never fails.
Now, hang me, but for all her art,
I find that I have gained her heart.
My proof is this: I plainly see
The case is just the same with me;
I curse her every hour sincerely,
Yet, hang me, but I love her dearly.

translated by JONATHAN SWIFT

NONE COULD EVER SAY THAT SHE

None could ever say that she,
Lesbia! was so loved by me.
Never all the world around
Faith so true as mine was found.
If no longer it endures
(Would it did!) the fault is yours.
I can never think again
Well of you: I try in vain.
But . . . be false . . . do what you will.—
Lesbia! I must love you still.

translated by WALTER SAVAGE LANDOR

DIANA GUARDETH OUR ESTATE

Diana guardeth our estate,
Girls and boys immaculate:
Boys and maidens pure of stain,
Be Diana our refrain.

O Latonia, pledge of love
Glorious to most glorious Jove,

Near the Delian olive-tree
Latonia gave thy life to thee,

That thou shouldst be forever queen
Of mountains and of forests green;
Of every deep glen's mystery;
Of all streams and their melody:

Women in travail ask their peace
From thee, our Lady of Release:
Thou art the Watcher of the Ways
Thou art the Moon with borrowed rays;

And as thy full or waning tide
Marks how the monthly seasons glide,
Thou, Goddess, sendest wealth of store
To bless the farmer's thrifty floor!

Whatever name delights thine ear,
By that name be thou hallowed here;
And as of old be good to us,
The lineage of Romulus!

translated by R. C. JEBB

SIRMIO

Gem of all isthmuses and isles that lie,
Fresh or salt water's children, in clear lake
Or ampler ocean: with what joy do I
Approach thee, Sirmio! Oh! am I awake,
Or dream that once again my eye beholds
Thee, and has looked its last on Thynian wolds?
Sweetest of sweets to me that pastime seems,

When the mind drops her burden: when—the pain
Of travel past—our own cot we regain,
And nestle on the pillow of our dreams!
'Tis this one thought that cheers us as we roam.
Hail, O fair Sirmio! Joy, thy Lord is here!
Joy too, ye waters of the Garda Mere!
And ring out, all ye laughter-peals of home.

translated by CHARLES STUART CALVERLEY

SUFFENUS, WHOM SO WELL YOU KNOW

Suffenus, whom so well you know,
My Varus, as a wit and beau,
Of smart address and smirking smile,
Will write you verses by the mile.
You cannot meet with daintier fare
Than title-page and binding are;
But when you once begin to read
You find it sorry stuff indeed,
And you are ready to cry out

Upon this beau—"O what a lout!"
No man on earth so proud as he
Of his own precious poetry,
Or knows such perfect bliss as when
He takes in hand that nibbled pen.
Have we not all some faults like these?
Are we not all Suffenuses?
In others the defect we find,
But cannot see our sack behind.

translated by WALTER SAVAGE LANDOR

ACME AND SEPTIMIUS

Whilst on Septimius' panting breast
(Meaning nothing less than rest)
Acme leaned her loving head,
Thus the pleased Septimius said.

My dearest Acme, if I be
Once alive, and love not thee
With a passion far above
All that e'er was callèd love,
In a Lybian desert may
I become some lion's prey,
Let him, Acme, let him tear
My breast, when Acme is not there.

The God of Love who stood to hear him,
(The God of Love was always near him)
Pleased and tickled with the sound,
Sneezed aloud, and all around
The little loves that waited by,
Bowed and blessed the augury.
Acme enflamed with what he said,
Reared her gently-bending head,
And her purple mouth with joy
Stretching to the delicious boy.
Twice (twice could scarce suffice)
She kissed his drunken, rolling eyes.

My little life, my all (said she)
So may we ever servants be
To this best god, and ne'er retain
Our hated liberty again,
So may thy passion last for me,
As I a passion have for thee,
Greater and fiercer much than can
Be conceived by thee a man.
Into my marrow is it gone,
Fixed and settled in the bone,
It reigns not only in my heart,
But runs, like life, through ev'ry part.
She spoke; the God of Love aloud
Sneezed again, and all the crowd

Of little loves that waited by,
Bowed and blessed the augury.
This good omen thus from heaven
Like a happy signal given,
Their loves and lives (all four) embrace,
And hand in hand run all the race.
To poor Septimius (who did now
Nothing else but Acme grow)
Acme's bosom was alone,
The whole world's imperial throne,
And to faithful Acme's mind
Septimius was all human kind.

If the gods would please to be
But advised for once by me,
I'd advise 'em when they spy
Any illustrious piety,
To reward her, if it be she;
To reward him, if it be he;
With such a husband, such a wife,
With Acme's and Septimius' life.

translated by ABRAHAM COWLEY

TELL ME, SPARROW

Tell me, sparrow, you darling of my darling,
whom she plays with and fondles in her bosom,
you who peck when she offers you a finger
(beak outthrust in a counterfeit of biting),
when that radiant star of my aspiring
turns towards you, as a pleasant little playmate,
one small bird, to console her when she suffers,
by your love to relieve her burning passion—
could I possibly play with you as she does,
could I lighten the pain that still torments me?

translated by GILBERT HIGHET

✳ MY WOMAN SAYS

My woman says that she'd prefer to marry no one
    but me, even if Jupiter asked for her love.
Ah yes: but what a woman says to an eager lover,
    write it on running water, write it on air.

translated by GILBERT HIGHET

✳ YOU POOR CATULLUS

You poor Catullus, don't be such a crass-brained fool!
All that is obviously lost, you must write off.
The sun shone brightly on you once, in days gone by,
when you would follow everywhere the girl led on—
the girl I loved as no girl ever will be loved.
Yes, then we had a thousand thousand pleasant games,
and you enjoyed them, and the girl did not hold back.

It's true: you lived in sunshine then, in times long gone.
Now she refuses. You then must refuse, you too:
don't follow when she runs, don't live a poor fool's life;
control your heart, endure it all, and be steel-hard.
Good-bye now, girl. Catullus has become steel-hard.
He will not chase you, beg for you against your will;
but you will surely suffer when you're asked no more.
You devil, you. What kind of life will you lead now?
Who will come courting you, and who will call you sweet?
Whom will you love, and whose girl will they say you are?
Whose lips will you be kissing now, with love-sharp bites?
No, no, Catullus, be determined: be steel-hard!

translated by GILBERT HIGHET

Vergil

PUBLIUS VERGILIUS MARO—70–19 B.C.

THE AENEID, BOOK I

Arms, and the man I sing, who, forced by fate,
And haughty Juno's unrelenting hate,
Expelled and exiled, left the Trojan shore.
Long labors, both by sea and land, he bore,
And in the doubtful war, before he won
The Latian realm, and built the destined town;
His banished gods restored to rites divine,
And settled sure succession in his line,
From whence the race of Alban fathers come,
And the long glories of majestic Rome.
  O Muse! the causes and the crimes relate;
What goddess was provoked, and whence her hate;
For what offense the Queen of Heav'n began
To persecute so brave, so just a man;
Involved his anxious life in endless cares,
Exposed to wants, and hurried into wars!
Can heav'nly minds such high resentment show,
Or exercise their spite in human woe?
  Against the Tiber's mouth, but far away,
An ancient town was seated on the sea;
A Tyrian colony; the people made
Stout for the war, and studious of their trade:
Carthage the name; beloved by Juno more
Than her own Argos, or the Samian shore.
Here stood her chariot; here, if Heav'n were kind,
The seat of awful empire she designed.
Yet she had heard an ancient rumor fly,
(Long cited by the people of the sky,)
That times to come should see the Trojan race
Her Carthage ruin, and her tow'rs deface;
Nor thus confined, the yoke of sov'reign sway
Should on the necks of all the nations lay.
She pondered this, and feared it was in fate;
Nor could forget the war she waged of late
For conqu'ring Greece against the Trojan state.
Besides, long causes working in her mind,
And secret seeds of envy, lay behind:
Deep graven in her heart the doom remained
Of partial Paris, and her form disdained;
The grace bestowed on ravished Ganymed,
Electra's glories, and her injured bed.
Each was a cause alone; and all combined
To kindle vengeance in her haughty mind.

For this, far distant from the Latian coast
She drove the remnants of the Trojan host;
And seven long years th' unhappy wand'ring train
Were tossed by storms, and scattered through the main.
Such time, such toil required the Roman name,
Such length of labor for so vast a frame.

Now scarce the Trojan fleet, with sails and oars,
Had left behind the fair Sicilian shores,
Ent'ring with cheerful shouts the wat'ry reign,
And plowing frothy furrows in the main;
When, lab'ring still with endless discontent,
The Queen of Heav'n did thus her fury vent:
"Then am I vanquished? must I yield?" said she,
"And must the Trojans reign in Italy?
So Fate will have it, and Jove adds his force;
Nor can my power divert their happy course.
Could angry Pallas, with revengeful spleen,
The Grecian navy burn, and drown the men?
She, for the fault of one offending foe,
The bolts of Jove himself presumed to throw:
With whirlwinds from beneath she tossed the ship,
And bare exposed the bosom of the deep;
Then, as an eagle gripes the trembling game,
The wretch, yet hissing with her father's flame,
She strongly seized, and with a burning wound
Transfixed, and naked, on a rock she bound.
But I, who walk in awful state above,
The majesty of heav'n, the sister wife of Jove,
For length of years my fruitless force employ
Against the thin remains of ruined Troy!
What nations now to Juno's power will pray,
Or off'rings on my slighted altars lay?"

Thus raged the goddess; and, with fury fraught,
The restless regions of the storms she sought,
Where, in a spacious cave of living stone,
The tyrant Æolus, from his airy throne,
With power imperial curbs the struggling winds,
And sounding tempests in dark prisons binds.
This way and that th' impatient captives tend,
And pressing for release, the mountains rend.
High in his hall th' undaunted monarch stands,
And shakes his scepter, and their rage commands;
Which did he not, their unresisted sway
Would sweep the world before them in their way;
Earth, air, and seas through empty space would roll,
And heav'n would fly before the driving soul.
In fear of this, the Father of the Gods
Confined their fury to those dark abodes,
And locked them safe within, oppressed with mountain loads;
Imposed a king, with arbitrary sway,
To loose their fetters, or their force allay.
To whom the suppliant queen her prayers addressed,
And thus the tenor of her suit expressed:
"O Æolus! for to thee the King of Heav'n
The power of tempest and of winds has giv'n;

Thy force alone their fury can restrain,
And smooth the waves, or swell the troubled main—
A race of wand'ring slaves, abhorred by me,
With prosp'rous passage cut the Tuscan sea;
To fruitful Italy their course they steer,
And for their vanquish'd gods design new temples there.
Raise all thy winds; with night involve the skies;
Sink or disperse my fatal enemies.
Twice seven, the charming daughters of the main,
Around my person wait, and bear my train:
Succeed my wish, and second my design;
The fairest, Deiopeia, shall be thine,
And make thee father of a happy line."
    To this the god: "'Tis yours, O queen, to will
The work which duty binds me to fulfil.
These airy kingdoms, and this wide command,
Are all the presents of your bounteous hand:
Yours is my sov'reign's grace; and, as your guest,
I sit with gods at their celestial feast;
Raise tempests at your pleasure, or subdue;
Dispose of empire, which I hold from you."
    He said, and hurled against the mountain side
His quiv'ring spear, and all the god applied.
The raging winds rush through the hollow wound,
And dance aloft in air, and skim along the ground;
Then, settling on the sea, the surges sweep,
Raise liquid mountains, and disclose the deep.
South, East, and West with mixed confusion roar,
And roll the foaming billows to the shore.
The cables crack; the sailors' fearful cries
Ascend; and sable night involves the skies;
And heav'n itself is ravished from their eyes.
Loud peals of thunder from the poles ensue;
Then flashing fires the transient light renew;
The face of things a frightful image bears,
And present death in various forms appears.
Struck with unusual fright, the Trojan chief,
With lifted hands and eyes, invokes relief;
And, "Thrice and four times happy those," he cried,
"That under Ilian walls before their parents died!
Tydides, bravest of the Grecian train!
Why could not I by that strong arm be slain,
And lie by noble Hector on the plain,
Or great Sarpedon, in those bloody fields
Where Simoïs rolls the bodies and the shields
Of heroes, whose dismembered hands yet bear
The dart aloft, and clench the pointed spear!"
    Thus while the pious prince his fate bewails,
Fierce Boreas drove against his flying sails,
And rent the sheets; the raging billows rise,
And mount the tossing vessel to the skies:
Nor can the shiv'ring oars sustain the blow;
The galley gives her side, and turns her prow;
While those astern, descending down the steep,
Through gaping waves behold the boiling deep.

Three ships were hurried by the southern blast,
And on the secret shelves with fury cast.
Those hidden rocks th' Ausonian sailors knew:
They called them altars, when they rose in view,
And showed their spacious backs above the flood.
Three more fierce Eurus, in his angry mood,
Dashed on the shallows of the moving sand,
And in mid ocean left them moored aland.
Orontes' bark, that bore the Lycian crew,
(A horrid sight!) ev'n in the hero's view,
From stem to stern by waves was overborne:
The trembling pilot, from his rudder torn,
Was headlong hurl'd; thrice round the ship was tossed,
Then bulged at once, and in the deep was lost;
And here and there above the waves were seen
Arms, pictures, precious goods, and floating men.
The stoutest vessel to the storm gave way,
And sucked through loosened planks the rushing sea.
Ilioneus was her chief: Alethes old,
Achates faithful, Abas young and bold,
Endured not less; their ships, with gaping seams,
Admit the deluge of the briny streams.
 Meantime imperial Neptune heard the sound
Of raging billows breaking on the ground.
Displeased, and fearing for his wat'ry reign,
He reared his awful head above the main,
Serene in majesty; then rolled his eyes
Around the space of earth, and seas, and skies.
He saw the Trojan fleet dispersed, distressed,
By stormy winds and wintry heav'n oppressed.
Full well the god his sister's envy knew,
And what her aims and what her arts pursue.
He summoned Eurus and the western blast,
And first an angry glance on both he cast;
Then thus rebuked: "Audacious winds! from whence
This bold attempt, this rebel insolence?
Is it for you to ravage seas and land,
Unauthorized by my supreme command?
To raise such mountains on the troubled main?
Whom I—but first 'tis fit the billows to restrain;
And then you shall be taught obedience to my reign.
Hence! to your lord my royal mandate bear—
The realms of ocean and the fields of air
Are mine, not his. By fatal lot to me
The liquid empire fell, and trident of the sea.
His power to hollow caverns is confined:
There let him reign, the jailer of the wind,
With hoarse commands his breathing subjects call,
And boast and bluster in his empty hall."
He spoke; and, while he spoke, he smoothed the sea,
Dispelled the darkness, and restored the day.
Cymothoe, Triton, and the sea-green train
Of beauteous nymphs, the daughters of the main,
Clear from the rocks the vessels with their hands:
The god himself with ready trident stands,

And opes the deep, and spreads the moving sands;
Then heaves them off the shoals. Where'er he guides
His finny coursers and in triumph rides,
The waves unruffle and the sea subsides
As, when in tumults rise th' ignoble crowd,
Mad are their motions, and their tongues are loud;
And stones and brands in rattling volleys fly,
And all the rustic arms that fury can supply;
If then some grave and pious man appear,
They hush their noise, and lend a list'ning ear;
He soothes with sober words their angry mood,
And quenches their innate desire of blood:
So, when the Father of the Flood appears,
And o'er the seas his sov'reign trident rears,
Their fury falls: he skims the liquid plains,
High on his chariot, and, with loosened reins,
Majestic moves along, and awful peace maintains.
The weary Trojans ply their shattered oars
To nearest land, and make the Libyan shores.
  Within a long recess there lies a bay:
An island shades it from the rolling sea,
And forms a port secure for ships to ride;
Broke by the jutting land, on either side,
In double streams the briny waters glide.
Betwixt two rows of rocks a sylvan scene
Appears above, and groves for ever green:
A grot is formed beneath, with mossy seats,
To rest the Nereids, and exclude the heats.
Down through the crannies of the living walls
The crystal streams descend in murm'ring falls:
No hawsers need to bind the vessels here,
Nor bearded anchors; for no storms they fear.
Seven ships within this happy harbor meet,
The thin remainders of the scattered fleet.
The Trojans, worn with toils, and spent with woes,
Leap on the welcome land, and seek their wished repose.
  First, good Achates, with repeated strokes
Of clashing flints, their hidden fire provokes:
Short flame succeeds; a bed of withered leaves
The dying sparkles in their fall receives:
Caught into life, in fiery fumes they rise,
And, fed with stronger food, invade the skies.
The Trojans, dropping wet, or stand around
The cheerful blaze, or lie along the ground:
Some dry their corn, infected with the brine,
Then grind with marbles, and prepare to dine.
Æneas climbs the mountain's airy brow,
And takes a prospect of the seas below,
If Capys thence, or Antheus he could spy,
Or see the streamers of Caïcus fly.
No vessels were in view; but, on the plain,
Three beamy stags command a lordly train
Of branching heads: the more ignoble throng
Attend their stately steps, and slowly graze along.
He stood; and, while secure they fed below,

He took the quiver and the trusty bow
Achates used to bear: the leaders first
He laid along, and then the vulgar pierced;
Nor ceased his arrows, till the shady plain
Seven mighty bodies with their blood distain.
For the seven ships he made an equal share,
And to the port returned, triumphant from the war.
The jars of gen'rous wine (Acestes' gift,
When his Trinacrian shores the navy left)
He set abroach, and for the feast prepared,
In equal portions with the venison shared.
Thus while he dealt it round, the pious chief
With cheerful words allayed the common grief:
"Endure, and conquer! Jove will soon dispose
To future good our past and present woes.
With me, the rocks of Scylla you have tried;
Th' inhuman Cyclops and his den defied.
What greater ills hereafter can you bear?
Resume your courage and dismiss your care.
An hour will come, with pleasure to relate
Your sorrows past, as benefits of Fate.
Through various hazards and events, we move
To Latium and the realms foredoomed by Jove.
Called to the seat (the promise of the skies)
Where Trojan kingdoms once again may rise,
Endure the hardships of your present state;
Live, and reserve yourselves for better fate."
　　These words he spoke, but spoke not from his heart;
His outward smiles concealed his inward smart.
The jolly crew, unmindful of the past,
The quarry share, their plenteous dinner haste.
Some strip the skin; some portion out the spoil;
The limbs, yet trembling, in the caldrons boil;
Some on the fire the reeking entrails broil.
Stretched on the grassy turf, at ease they dine,
Restore their strength with meat, and cheer their souls with
　　wine.
Their hunger thus appeased, their care attends
The doubtful fortune of their absent friends:
Alternate hopes and fears their minds possess,
Whether to deem them dead, or in distress.
Above the rest, Æneas mourns the fate
Of brave Orontes, and th' uncertain state
Of Gyas, Lycus, and of Amycus.
The day, but not their sorrows, ended thus.
　　When, from aloft, almighty Jove surveys
Earth, air, and shores, and navigable seas,
At length on Libyan realms he fixed his eyes—
Whom, pond'ring thus on human miseries,
When Venus saw, she with a lowly look,
Not free from tears, her heav'nly sire bespoke:
　　"O King of Gods and Men! whose awful hand
Disperses thunder on the seas and land,
Disposing all with absolute command;
How could my pious son thy pow'r incense?

Or what, alas! is vanished Troy's offense?
Our hope of Italy not only lost,
On various seas by various tempests tossed,
But shut from ev'ry shore, and barred from ev'ry coast.
You promised once, a progeny divine
Of Romans, rising from the Trojan line,
In after times should hold the world in awe,
And to the land and ocean give the law.
How is your doom reversed, which eased my care
When Troy was ruined in that cruel war?
Then fates to fates I could oppose; but now,
When Fortune still pursues her former blow,
What can I hope? What worse can still succeed?
What end of labors has your will decreed?
Antenor, from the midst of Grecian hosts,
Could pass secure, and pierce th' Illyrian coasts,
Where, rolling down the steep, Timavus raves
And through nine channels disembogues his waves.
At length he founded Padua's happy seat,
And gave his Trojans a secure retreat;
There fixed their arms, and there renewed their name,
And there in quiet rules, and crowned with fame.
But we, descended from your sacred line,
Entitled to your heav'n and rites divine,
Are banished earth; and, for the wrath of one,
Removed from Latium and the promised throne.
Are these our scepters? these our due rewards?
And is it thus that Jove his plighted faith regards?"
  To whom the Father of th' immortal race,
Smiling with that serene indulgent face,
With which he drives the clouds and clears the skies,
First gave a holy kiss; then thus replies:
  "Daughter, dismiss thy fears: to thy desire
The fates of thine are fixed, and stand entire.
Thou shalt behold thy wished Lavinian walls;
And, ripe for heav'n, when fate Æneas calls,
Then shalt thou bear him up, sublime, to me:
No councils have reversed my firm decree.
And, lest new fears disturb thy happy state,
Know, I have searched the mystic rolls of Fate:
Thy son (nor is th' appointed season far)
In Italy shall wage successful war,
Shall tame fierce nations in the bloody field,
And sov'reign laws impose, and cities build,
Till, after ev'ry foe subdued, the sun
Thrice through the signs his annual race shall run!
This is his time prefixed. Ascanium then,
Now called Iülus, shall begin his reign.
He thirty rolling years the crown shall wear,
Then from Lavinium shall the seat transfer,
And, with hard labor, Alba Longa build,
The throne with his succession shall be filled
Three hundred circuits more: then shall be seen
Ilia the fair, a priestess and a queen,
Who, full of Mars, in time, with kindly throes,

Shall at a birth two goodly boys disclose.
The royal babes a tawny wolf shall drain:
Then Romulus his grandsire's throne shall gain,
Of martial towers the founder shall become,
The people Romans call, the city Rome.
To them no bounds of empire I assign,
Nor term of years to their immortal line.
Ev'n haughty Juno, who, with endless broils,
Earth, seas, and heav'n, and Jove himself turmoils;
At length atoned, her friendly power shall join,
To cherish and advance the Trojan line.
The subject world shall Rome's dominion own.
And, prostrate, shall adore the nation of the gown.
An age is ripening in revolving fate
When Troy shall overturn the Grecian state,
And sweet revenge her conqu'ring sons shall call,
To crush the people that conspired her fall.
Then Caesar from the Julian stock shall rise,
Whose empire ocean, and whose fame the skies
Alone shall bound; whom, fraught with eastern spoils,
Our heav'n, the just reward of human toils,
Securely shall repay with rites divine;
And incense shall ascend before his sacred shrine.
Then dire debate and impious war shall cease,
And the stern age be softened into peace:
Then banished Faith shall once again return,
And Vestal fires in hallowed temples burn;
And Remus with Quirinus shall sustain
The righteous laws, and fraud and force restrain.
Janus himself before his fane shall wait,
And keep the dreadful issues of his gate,
With bolts and iron bars: within remains
Imprisoned Fury, bound in brazen chains;
High on a trophy raised, of useless arms,
He sits, and threats the world with vain alarms."

He said, and sent Cyllenius with command
To free the ports, and ope the Punic land
To Trojan guests; lest, ignorant of fate,
The queen might force them from her town and state.
Down from the steep of heav'n Cyllenius flies,
And cleaves with all his wings the yielding skies.
Soon on the Libyan shore descends the god,
Performs his message, and displays his rod:
The surly murmurs of the people cease;
And, as the fates required, they give the peace:
The queen herself suspends the rigid laws,
The Trojans pities, and protects their cause.

Meantime, in shades of night Æneas lies:
Care seized his soul, and sleep forsook his eyes.
But, when the sun restored the cheerful day,
He rose, the coast and country to survey,
Anxious and eager to discover more.
It looked a wild uncultivated shore;
But, whether humankind, or beasts alone
Possessed the new-found region, was unknown.

Beneath a ledge of rocks his fleet he hides:
Tall trees surround the mountain's shady sides;
The bending brow above a safe retreat provides.
Armed with two pointed darts, he leaves his friends,
And true Achates on his steps attends.
Lo! in the deep recesses of the wood,
Before his eyes his goddess mother stood:
A huntress in her habit and her mien;
Her dress a maid, her air confessed a queen.
Bare were her knees, and knots her garments bind;
Loose was her hair, and wantoned in the wind;
Her hand sustained a bow; her quiver hung behind.
She seemed a virgin of the Spartan blood:
With such array Harpalyce bestrode
Her Thracian courser and outstripped the rapid flood.
"Ho, strangers! have you lately seen," she said,
"One of my sisters, like myself arrayed,
Who crossed the lawn, or in the forest strayed?
A painted quiver at her back she bore;
Varied with spots, a lynx's hide she wore;
And at full cry pursued the tusky boar."
  Thus Venus: thus her son replied again:
"None of your sisters have we heard or seen,
O virgin! or what other name you bear
Above that style—O more than mortal fair!
Your voice and mien celestial birth betray!
If, as you seem, the sister of the day,
Or one at least of chaste Diana's train,
Let not an humble suppliant sue in vain;
But tell a stranger, long in tempests tossed,
What earth we tread, and who commands the coast?
Then on your name shall wretched mortals call,
And offered victims at your altars fall."
"I dare not," she replied, "assume the name
Of goddess, or celestial honors claim:
For Tyrian virgins bows and quivers bear,
And purple buskins o'er their ankles wear.
Know, gentle youth, in Libyan lands you are
A people rude in peace, and rough in war.
The rising city, which from far you see,
Is Carthage, and a Tyrian colony.
Phoenician Dido rules the growing state,
Who fled from Tyre, to shun her brother's hate.
Great were her wrongs, her story full of fate;
Which I will sum in short. Sichæus, known
For wealth, and brother to the Punic throne,
Possessed fair Dido's bed; and either heart
At once was wounded with an equal dart.
Her father gave her, yet a spotless maid;
Pygmalion then the Tyrian scepter sway'd;
One who contemned divine and human laws.
Then strife ensued, and cursed gold the cause.
The monarch, blinded with desire of wealth,
With steel invades his brother's life by stealth;
Before the sacred altar made him bleed,

And long from her concealed the cruel deed.
Some tale, some new pretense, he daily coined,
To soothe his sister, and delude her mind.
At length, in dead of night, the ghost appears
Of her unhappy lord: the specter stares,
And, with erected eyes, his bloody bosom bares.
The cruel altars and his fate he tells,
And the dire secret of his house reveals,
Then warns the widow, with her household gods,
To seek refuge in remote abodes.
Last, to support her in so long a way,
He shows her where his hidden treasure lay.
Admonished thus, and seized with mortal fright,
The queen provides companions of her flight;
They meet, and all combine to leave the state,
Who hate the tyrant, or who fear his hate.
They seize a fleet, which ready rigged they find;
Nor is Pygmalion's treasure left behind.
The vessels, heavy laden, put to sea
With prosp'rous winds; a woman leads the way.
I know not, if by stress of weather driven,
Or was their fatal course disposed by Heav'n;
At last they landed, where from far your eyes
May view the turrets of new Carthage rise;
There bought a space of ground, which (Byrsa called,
From the bull's hide) they first inclosed, and walled,
But whence are you? what country claims your birth?
What seek you, strangers, on our Libyan earth?"
　　To whom, with sorrow streaming from his eyes,
And deeply sighing, thus her son replies:
"Could you with patience hear, or I relate,
O nymph, the tedious annals of our fate!
Through such a train of woes if I should run,
The day would sooner than the tale be done!
From ancient Troy, by force expelled, we came—
If you by chance have heard the Trojan name.
On various seas by various tempests tossed,
At length we landed on your Libyan coast.
The good Æneas am I called—a name,
While Fortune favored, not unknown to fame.
My household gods, companions of my woes,
With pious care I rescued from our foes.
To fruitful Italy my course was bent;
And from the King of Heav'n is my descent.
With twice ten sail I crossed the Phrygian sea;
Fate and my mother goddess fled my way.
Scarce sev'n, the thin remainders of my fleet,
From storms preserved, within your harbor meet.
Myself distressed, an exile, and unknown,
Debarred from Europe, and from Asia thrown,
In Libyan deserts wander thus alone."
　　His tender parent could no longer bear;
But, interposing, sought to soothe his care.
"Whoe'er you are—not unbelov'd by Heav'n,
Since on our friendly shore your ships are driv'n—

Have courage: to the gods permit the rest,
And to the queen expose your just request.
Now take this earnest of success, for more:
Your scattered fleet is join'd upon the shore;
The winds are changed, your friends from danger free;
Or I renounce my skill in augury.
Twelve swans behold in beauteous order move,
And stoop with closing pinions from above;
Whom late the bird of Jove had driv'n along,
And through the clouds pursued the scatt'ring throng:
Now, all united in a goodly team,
They skim the ground, and seek the quiet stream.
As they, with joy returning, clap their wings,
And ride the circuit of the skies in rings;
Not otherwise your ships, and ev'ry friend,
Already hold the port, or with swift sails descend.
No more advice is needful; but pursue
The path before you, and the town in view."
    Thus having said, she turned, and made appear
Her neck refulgent, and disheveled hair,
Which, flowing from her shoulders, reached the ground,
And widely spread ambrosial scents around:
In length of train descends her sweeping gown;
And, by her graceful walk, the Queen of Love is known,
The prince pursued the parting deity
With words like these: "Ah! whither do you fly?
Unkind and cruel! to deceive your son
In borrowed shapes, and his embrace to shun;
Never to bless my sight, but thus unknown;
And still to speak in accents not your own."
Against the goddess these complaints he made,
But took the path, and her commands obeyed.
They march obscure; for Venus kindly shrouds
With mists their persons, and involves in clouds,
That, thus unseen, their passage none might stay,
Or force to tell the causes of their way.
This part performed, the goddess flies sublime
To visit Paphos and her native clime;
Where garlands, ever green and ever fair,
With vows are offered, and with solemn prayer:
A hundred altars in her temple smoke;
A thousand bleeding hearts her power invoke.
    They climb the next ascent, and, looking down,
Now at a nearer distance view the town.
The prince with wonder sees the stately towers,
Which late were huts and shepherds' homely bowers,
The gates and streets; and hears, from ev'ry part,
The noise and busy concourse of the mart.
The roiling Tyrians on each other call
To ply their labor: some extend the wall;
Some build the citadel; the brawny throng
Or dig, or push unwieldly stones along.
Some for their dwellings choose a spot of ground,
Which, first designed, with ditches they surround.
Some laws ordain; and some attend the choice

Of holy senates, and elect by voice.
Here some design a mole, while others there
Lay deep foundations for a theater;
From marble quarries mighty columns hew,
For ornaments of scenes, and future view.
Such is their toil, and such their busy pains,
As exercise the bees in flow'ry plains,
When winter past, and summer scarce begun,
Invites them forth to labor in the sun;
Some lead their youth abroad, while some condense
Their liquid store, and some in cells dispense;
Some at the gate stand ready to receive
The golden burthen, and their friends relieve;
All, with united force, combine to drive
The lazy drones from the laborious hive:
With envy stung, they view each other's deeds;
The fragrant work with diligence proceeds.
"Thrice happy you, whose walls already rise!"
Æneas said, and, viewed, with lifted eyes,
Their lofty towers; then, ent'ring at the gate,
Concealed in clouds (prodigious to relate)
He mixed, unmarked, among the busy throng,
Borne by the tide, and passed unseen along.
 Full in the center of the town there stood,
Thick set with trees, a venerable wood.
The Tyrians, landing near this holy ground,
And digging here, a prosp'rous omen found:
From under earth a courser's head they drew,
Their growth and future fortune to foreshew.
This fated sign their foundress Juno gave,
Of a soil fruitful, and a people brave.
Sidonian Dido here with solemn state
Did Juno's temple build, and consecrate,
Enriched with gifts, and with a golden shrine;
But more the goddess made the place divine.
On brazen steps the marble threshold rose,
And brazen plates the cedar beams inclose:
The rafters are with brazen cov'rings crowned;
The lofty doors on brazen hinges sound.
What first Æneas in this place beheld,
Revived his courage, and his fear expelled.
For while, expecting there the queen, he raised
His wond'ring eyes, and round the temple gazed,
Admired the fortune of the rising town,
The striving artists, and their arts' renown;
He saw, in order painted on the wall,
Whatever did unhappy Troy befall:
The wars that fame around the world had blown,
All to the life, and ev'ry leader known.
There Agamemnon, Priam here, he spies,
And fierce Achilles, who both kings defies.
He stopped, and weeping said: "O friend! ev'n here
The monuments of Trojan woes appear!
Our known disasters fill ev'n foreign lands:
See there, where old unhappy Priam stands!

Ev'n the mute walls relate the warrior's fame,
And Trojan griefs the Tyrians' pity claim."
He said (his tears a ready passage find),
Devouring what he saw so well designed,
And with an empty picture fed his mind:
For there he saw the fainting Grecians yield,
And here the trembling Trojans quit the field,
Pursued by fierce Achilles through the plain,
On his high chariot driving o'er the slain.
The tents of Rhesus next his grief renew,
By their white sails betrayed to nightly view;
And wakeful Diomede, whose cruel sword
The sentries slew, nor spared their slumb'ring lord,
Then took the fiery steeds, ere yet the food
Of Troy they taste, or drink the Xanthian flood.
Elsewhere he saw where Troilus defied
Achilles, and unequal combat tried;
Then, where the boy disarmed, with loosened reins,
Was by his horses hurried o'er the plains,
Hung by the neck and hair, and dragged around:
The hostile spear, yet sticking in his wound,
With tracks of blood inscribed the dusty ground.
Meantime the Trojan dames, oppressed with woe,
To Pallas' fane in long procession go,
In hopes to reconcile their heav'nly foe.
They weep, they beat their breasts, they rend their hair,
And rich embroidered vests for presents bear;
But the stern goddess stands unmoved with prayer.
Thrice round the Trojan walls Achilles drew
The corpse of Hector, whom in fight he slew.
Here Priam sues; and there, for sums of gold,
The lifeless body of his son is sold.
So sad an object, and so well expressed,
Drew sighs and groans from the grieved hero's breast,
To see the figure of his lifeless friend,
And his old sire his helpless hand extend.
Himself he saw amidst the Grecian train,
Mixed in the bloody battle on the plain;
And swarthy Memnon in his arms he knew,
His pompous ensigns, and his Indian crew.
Penthosilea there, with haughty grace,
Leads to the wars an Amazonian race:
In their right hands a pointed dart they wield;
The left, for ward, sustains the lunar shield.
Athwart her breast a golden belt she throws,
Amidst the press alone provokes a thousand foes,
And dares her maiden arms to manly force oppose.
    Thus while the Trojan prince employs his eyes,
Fixed on the walls with wonder and surprise,
The beauteous Dido, with a num'rous train
And pomp of guards, ascends the sacred fane.
Such on Eurotas' banks, or Cynthus' height,
Diana seems; and so she charms the sight,
When in the dance the graceful goddess leads
The choir of nymphs, and overtops their heads:

Known by her quiver, and her lofty mien,
She walks majestic, and she looks their queen;
Latona sees her shine above the rest,
And feeds with secret joy her silent breast.
Such Dido was; with such becoming state,
Amidst the crowd, she walks serenely great.
Their labor to her future sway she speeds,
And passing with a gracious glance proceeds;
Then mounts the throne, high placed before the shrine:
In crowds around, the swarming people join.
She takes petitions, and dispenses laws,
Hears and determines ev'ry private cause;
Their tasks in equal portions she divides,
And, where unequal, there by lots decides.
Another way by chance Æneas bends
His eyes, and unexpected sees his friends,
Antheus, Sergestus grave, Cloanthus strong,
And at their backs a mighty Trojan throng,
Whom late the tempest on the billows tossed,
And widely scattered on another coast.
The prince, unseen, surprised with wonder stands,
And longs, with joyful haste, to join their hands;
But doubtful of the wished event, he stays,
And from the hollow cloud his friends surveys,
Impatient till they hold their present state,
And where they left their ships, and what their fate,
And why they came, and what was their request;
For these were sent, commissioned by the rest,
To sue for leave to land their sickly men,
And gain admission to the gracious queen.
Ent'ring, with cries they filled the holy fane;
Then thus, with lowly voice, Ilioneus began:
    "O queen! indulged by favor of the gods
To found an empire in these new abodes,
To build a town, with statutes to restrain
The wild inhabitants beneath thy reign,
We wretched Trojans, tossed on ev'ry shore,
From sea to sea, thy clemency implore.
Forbid the fires our shipping to deface!
Receive th' unhappy fugitives to grace,
And spare the remnant of a pious race!
We come not with design of wasteful prey,
To drive the country, force the swains away:
Nor such our strength, nor such is our desire;
The vanquished dare not to such thoughts aspire.
A land there is, Hesperia named of old
(The soil is fruitful, and the men are bold—
Th' Œnotrians held it once), by common fame
Now called Italia, from the leader's name.
To that sweet region was our voyage bent,
When winds and ev'ry warring element
Disturbed our course, and, far from sight of land,
Cast our torn vessels on the moving sand:
The sea came on; the South, with mighty roar,
Dispersed and dashed the rest upon the rocky shore.

Those few you see escaped the storm, and fear,
Unless you interpose, a shipwreck here.
What men, what monsters, what inhuman race,
What laws, what barb'rous customs of the place,
Shut up a desert shore to drowning men,
And drive us to the cruel seas again?
If our hard fortune no compassion draws,
Nor hospitable rights, nor human laws,
The gods are just, and will revenge our cause.
Æneas was our prince: a juster lord,
Or nobler warrior, never drew a sword;
Observant of the right, religious of his word.
If yet he lives, and draws this vital air,
Nor we, his friends, of safety shall despair;
Nor you, great queen, these offices repent,
Which he will equal, and perhaps augment.
We want not cities, nor Sicilian coasts,
Where King Acestes Trojan lineage boasts.
Permit our ships a shelter on your shores,
Refitted from your woods with planks and oars,
That, if our prince be safe, we may renew
Our destined course, and Italy pursue.
But if, O best of men, the Fates ordain
That thou art swallowed in the Libyan main,
And if our young Iülus be no more,
Dismiss our navy from your friendly shore,
That we to good Acestes may return,
And with our friends our common losses mourn."
Thus spoke Ilioneus: the Trojan crew
With cries and clamors his request renew.

The modest queen a while, with downcast eyes;
Pondered the speech; then briefly thus replies:
"Trojans, dismiss your fears; my cruel fate,
And doubts attending an unsettled state,
Force me to guard my coast from foreign foes.
Who has not heard the story of your woes,
The name and fortune of your native place,
The fame and valor of the Phrygian race?
We Tyrians are not so devoid of sense,
Nor so remote from Phoebus' influence.
Whether to Latian shores your course is bent,
Or, driv'n by tempests from your first intent,
You see the good Acestes' government,
Your men shall be received, your fleet repaired,
And sail, with ships of convoy for your guard:
Or, would you stay, and join your friendly powers
To raise and to defend the Tyrian towers,
My wealth, my city, and myself are yours.
And would to Heav'n, the storm, you felt, would bring
On Carthaginian coasts your wand'ring king.
My people shall, by my command, explore
The ports and creeks of ev'ry winding shore,
And towns, and wilds, and shady woods, in quest
Of so renowned and so desired a guest."
Raised in his mind the Trojan hero stood,

And longed to break from out his ambient cloud:
Achates found it, and thus urged his way:
"From whence, O goddess-born, this long delay?
What more can you desire, your welcome sure,
Your fleet in safety, and your friends secure?
One only wants; and him we saw in vain
Oppose the storm, and swallowed in the main.
Orontes in his fate our forfeit paid;
The rest agrees with what your mother said."
Scarce had he spoken, when the cloud gave way,
The mists flew upward and dissolved in day.
The Trojan chief appeared in open sight,
August in visage, and serenely bright.
His mother goddess, with her hands divine,
Had formed his curling locks, and made his temples shine,
And giv'n his rolling eyes a sparkling grace,
And breathed a youthful vigor on his face;
Like polished iv'ry, beauteous to behold,
Or Parian marble, when enchased in gold:
Thus radiant from the circling cloud he broke,
And thus with manly modesty he spoke:
"He whom you seek am I; by tempests tossed,
And saved from shipwreck on your Libyan coast;
Presenting, gracious queen, before your throne,
A prince that owes his life to you alone.
Fair majesty, the refuge and redress
Of those whom fate pursues, and wants oppress,
You, who your pious offices employ
To save the relics of abandon'd Troy;
Receive the shipwrecked on your friendly shore,
With hospitable rites relieve the poor;
Associate in your town a wand'ring train,
And strangers in your palace entertain:
What thanks can wretched fugitives return,
Who, scattered through the world, in exile mourn?
The gods, if gods to goodness are inclined;
If acts of mercy touch their heav'nly mind,
And, more than all the gods, your gen'rous heart,
Conscious of worth, requite its own desert!
In you this age is happy, and this earth,
And parents more than mortal gave you birth.
While rolling rivers into seas shall run,
And round the space of heav'n the radiant sun;
While trees the mountain tops with shades supply,
Your honor, name, and praise shall never die.
Whate'er abode my fortune has assigned,
Your image shall be present in my mind."
Thus having said, he turned with pious haste,
And joyful his expecting friends embraced:
With his right hand Ilioneus was graced,
Serestus with his left; then to his breast
Cloanthus and the noble Gyas pressed;
And so by turns descended to the rest.
    The Tyrian queen stood fixed upon his face,
Pleased with his motions, ravished with his grace;

Admired his fortunes, more admired the man;
Then recollected stood, and thus began:
"What fate, O goddess-born! what angry powers
Have cast you shipwrecked on our barren shores?
Are you the great Æneas, known to fame,
Who from celestial seed your lineage claim?
The same Æneas whom fair Venus bore
To famed Anchises on th' Idæan shore?
It calls into my mind, who then a child,
When Teucer came, from Salamis exiled,
And sought my father's aid, to be restored:
My father Belus then with fire and sword
Invaded Cyprus, made the region bare,
And, conqu'ring, finished the successful war.
From him the Trojan siege I understood,
The Grecian chiefs, and your illustrious blood.
Your foe himself the Dardan valor praised,
And his own ancestry from Trojans raised.
Enter, my noble guest, and you shall find,
If not a costly welcome, yet a kind:
For I myself, like you, have been distressed,
Till Heav'n afforded me this place of rest;
Like you, an alien in a land unknown,
I learn to pity woes so like my own."
She said, and to the palace led her guest;
Then offer'd incense, and proclaimed a feast.
Nor yet less careful for her absent friends,
Twice ten fat oxen to the ships she sends;
Besides a hundred boars, a hundred lambs,
With bleating cries, attend their milky dams;
And jars of gen'rous wine and spacious bowls
She gives, to cheer the sailors' drooping souls.
Now purple hangings clothe the palace walls,
And sumptuous feasts are made in splendid halls:
On Tyrian carpets, richly wrought, they dine;
With loads of massy plate the sideboards shine,
And antique vases, all of gold embossed
(The gold itself inferior to the cost),
Of curious work, where on the sides were seen
The fights and figures of illustrious men,
From their first founder to the present queen.

    The good Æneas, whose paternal care
Iülus' absence could no longer bear,
Dispatched Achates to the ships in haste,
To give a glad relation of the past,
And, fraught with precious gifts, to bring the boy,
Snatched from the ruins of unhappy Troy:
A robe of tissue, stiff with golden wire;
An upper vest, once Helen's rich attire,
From Argos by the famed adultress brought,
With golden flowers and winding foliage wrought,
Her mother Leda's present, when she came
To ruin Troy and set the world on flame;
The scepter Priam's eldest daughter bore,
Her orient necklace, and the crown she wore;

Of double texture, glorious to behold,
One order set with gems, and one with gold.
Instructed thus, the wise Achates goes,
And in his diligence his duty shows.
 But Venus, anxious for her son's affairs,
New counsels tries, and new designs prepares
That Cupid should assume the shape and face
Of sweet Ascanius, and the sprightly grace;
Should bring the presents, in her nephew's stead,
And in Eliza's veins the gentle poison shed:
For much she fear'd the Tyrians, double-tongued,
And knew the town to Juno's care belonged.
These thoughts by night her golden slumbers broke,
And thus alarmed, to winged Love she spoke:
"My son, my strength, whose mighty power alone
Controls the Thund'rer on his awful throne,
To thee thy much-afflicted mother flies,
And on thy succor and thy faith relies.
Thou know'st, my son, how Jove's revengeful wife,
By force and fraud, attempts thy brother's life;
And often hast thou mourned with me his pains.
Him Dido now with blandishment detains;
But I suspect the town where Juno reigns.
For this 'tis needful to prevent her art,
And fire with love the proud Phoenician's heart:
A love so violent, so strong, so sure,
As neither age can change, nor art can cure.
How this may be performed, now take my mind:
Ascanius by his father is designed
To come, with presents laden, from the port,
To gratify the queen, and gain the court.
I mean to plunge the boy in pleasing sleep,
And, ravished, in Idalian bowers to keep,
Or high Cythera, that the sweet deceit
May pass unseen, and none prevent the cheat.
Take thou his form and shape. I beg the grace
But only for a night's revolving space:
Thyself a boy, assume a boy's dissembled face;
That when, amidst the fervor of the feast,
The Tyrian hugs and fonds thee on her breast,
And with sweet kisses in her arms constrains,
Thou may'st infuse thy venom in her veins."
The God of Love obeys, and sets aside
His bow and quiver, and his plumy pride;
He walks Iülus in his mother's sight,
And in the sweet resemblance takes delight.
 The goddess then to young Ascanius flies,
And in a pleasing slumber seals his eyes:
Lulled in her lap, amidst a train of Loves,
She gently bears him to her blissful groves,
Then with a wreath of myrtle crowns his head,
And softly lays him on a flow'ry bed.
Cupid meantime assum'd his form and face,
Foll'wing Achates with a shorter pace,
And brought the gifts. The queen already sate

Amidst the Trojan lords, in shining state,
High on a golden bed: her princely guest
Was next her side; in order sate the rest.
Then canisters with bread are heaped on high;
Th' attendants water for their hands supply,
And, having washed, with silken towels dry.
Next fifty handmaids in long order bore
The censers, and with fumes the gods adore:
Then youths, and virgins twice as many, join
To place the dishes, and to serve the wine.
The Tyrian train, admitted to the feast,
Approach, and on the painted couches rest.
All on the Trojan gifts with wonder gaze,
But view the beauteous boy with more amaze,
His rosy-colored cheeks, his radiant eyes,
His motions, voice, and shape, and all the god's disguise;
Nor pass unpraised the vest and veil divine,
Which wand'ring foliage and rich flowers entwine.
But, far above the rest, the royal dame,
(Already doom'd to love's disastrous flame),
With eyes insatiate, and tumultuous joy,
Beholds the presents, and admires the boy.
The guileful god about the hero long,
With children's play, and false embraces, hung;
Then sought the queen; she took him to her arms
With greedy pleasure, and devoured his charms.
Unhappy Dido little thought what guest,
How dire a god, she drew so near her breast;
But he, not mindless of his mother's pray'r,
Works in the pliant bosom of the fair,
And molds her heart anew, and blots her former care.
The dead is to the living love resigned;
And all Æneas enters in her mind.
　　Now, when the rage of hunger was appeased
The meat removed, and ev'ry guest was pleas'd,
The golden bowls with sparkling wine are crowned,
And through the palace cheerful cries resound.
From gilded roofs depending lamps display
Nocturnal beams, that emulate the day.
A golden bowl, that shone with gems divine,
The queen commanded to be crowned with wine:
The bowl that Belus used, and all the Tyrian line.
Then, silence through the hall proclaimed, she spoke:
"O hospitable Jove! we thus invoke,
With solemn rites, thy sacred name and power;
Bless to both nations this auspicious hour!
So may the Trojan and the Tyrian line
In lasting concord from this day combine.
Thou, Bacchus, god of joys and friendly cheer,
And gracious Juno, both be present here!
And you, my lords of Tyre, your vows address
To Heav'n with mine, to ratify the peace."
The goblet then she took, with nectar crowned,
(Sprinkling the first libations on the ground),
And raised it to her mouth with sober grace;

Then, sipping, offered to the next in place.
'Twas Bitias whom she called, a thirsty soul;
He took the challenge, and embraced the bowl,
With pleasure swilled the gold, nor ceased to draw,
Till he the bottom of the brimmer saw,
The goblet goes around: Iopas brought
His golden lyre, and sung what ancient Atlas taught:
The various labors of the wand'ring moon,
And whence proceed th' eclipses of the sun;
Th' original of men and beasts; and whence
The rains arise, and fires their warmth dispense,
And fixed and erring stars dispose their influence;
What shakes the solid earth; what cause delays
The summer nights and shortens winter days.
With peals of shouts the Tyrians praise the song;
Those peals are echoed by the Trojan throng.
The unhappy queen with talk prolonged the night,
And drank large draughts of love with vast delight;
Of Priam much enquired, of Hector more;
Then asked what arms the swarthy Memnon wore,
What troops he landed on the Trojan shore;
The steeds of Diomede varied the discourse,
And fierce Achilles, with his matchless force;
At length, as fate and her ill stars required,
To hear the series of the war desired.
"Relate at large, my godlike guest," she said,
"The Grecian stratagems, the town betrayed:
The fatal issue of so long a war,
Your flight, your wand'rings, and your woes, declare;
For, since on ev'ry sea, on ev'ry coast,
Your men have been distressed, your navy tossed,
Seven times the sun has either tropic viewed,
The winter banished, and the spring renewed."

translated by JOHN DRYDEN

Horace

QUINTUS HORATIUS FLACCUS—65-8 B.C.

WHAT SLIM ELEGANT YOUTH

Odes, I, 5

What slim elegant youth, drenched in effusive scent,
now sits close to your side, Pyrrha, in some recess
    rich with many a rose-bloom?
  Who loves smoothing your yellow hair,
chic yet daintily plain? How many gods profaned,
what indelible vows he will lament, and oh,
    what dark hurricane-lashed seas
  he will watch with a pallid cheek!
Poor fool, golden he thinks you will for ever be,
heart-free always, he hopes, always adorable—
    yet knows not the deceitful
  off-shore squalls. To a novice, you
shine too temptingly bright. Here on the temple wall
one small tablet of mine, offering up my clothes
    (all I saved from a shipwreck),
  says Thank God, that I just escaped.

               translated by GILBERT HIGHET

WHAT SLENDER YOUTH

Odes, I, 5

What slender youth, bedewed with liquid odors,
Courts thee on roses in some pleasant cave,
    Pyrrha? For whom bind'st thou
    In wreaths thy golden hair,
Plain in thy neatness? O how oft shall he
Of faith and changed gods complain, and seas
    Rough with black winds, and storms
    Unwonted shall admire!
Who now enjoys thee credulous, all gold,
Who, always vacant, always amiable
    Hopes thee, of flattering gales
    Unmindful. Hapless they
To whom thou untried seem'st fair. Me, in my vowed
Picture, the sacred wall declares to have hung
    My dank and dropping weeds
    To the stern god of sea.

               translated by JOHN MILTON

WHILST, LYDIA, I WAS LOVED OF THEE

Odes, III, 9

HORACE.   Whilst, Lydia, I was loved of
thee,
And 'bout thy ivory neck no youth
did fling
His arms more acceptably free,
I thought me richer than the
Persian king.

LYDIA.   Whilst Horace loved no mistress
more,
Nor after Chloe did his Lydia
sound;
In name I went all names before,
The Roman Ilia was not more
renowned.

HORACE.   'Tis true, I'm Thracian Chloe's I,
Who sings so sweet, and with such
cunning plays,
As, for her, I'd not fear to die,
So fate would give her life, and
longer days.

LYDIA.   And I am mutually on fire
With gentle Calais, Thurine
Ornith's son,
For whom I doubly would expire,
So fate would let the boy a long
thread run.

HORACE.   But say old love return should
make,
And us disjoined force to her
brazen yoke;
That I bright Chloe off should
shake,
And to left Lydia now the gate
stood ope?

LYDIA.   Though he be fairer than a star;
Thou lighter than the bark of any
tree,
And than rough Adria angrier far;
Yet would I wish to love, live, die
with thee.

translated by BEN JONSON

BEHOLD YON MOUNTAIN'S HOARY HEIGHT

Odes, I, 9

Behold yon mountain's hoary height,
  Made higher with new mounts of snow;
Again behold the winter's weight
  Oppress the laboring woods below:
And streams with icy fetters bound,
Benumbed and cramped to solid ground.

With well-heaped logs dissolve the cold,
  And feed the genial hearth with fires;
Produce the wine that makes us bold,
  And sprightly wit and love inspires:
For what hereafter shall betide,
God, if 'tis worth his care, provide.

Let him alone, with what he made,
  To toss and turn the world below;
At his command the storms invade;
  The winds by his commission blow;
Till with a nod he bids them cease,
And then the calm returns, and all is peace.

To-morrow and her works defy,
  Lay hold upon the present hour,
And snatch the pleasures passing by,
  To put them out of fortune's power:
Nor love, nor love's delights disdain;
Whate'er thou get'st to-day, is gain.

Secure those golden early joys,
  That youth unsoured with sorrows bears,
Ere with'ring time the taste destroys,
  With sickness and unwieldy years.
This is the time to be possessed;
The best is but in season best.

Th' appointed hour of promised bliss,
  The pleasing whisper in the dark,
The half unwilling willing kiss,
  The laugh that guides thee to the mark,
When the kind nymph would coyness feign,
And hides but to be found again;
These, these are joys the gods for youth ordain.

translated by JOHN DRYDEN

TO SALLY

Odes, I, 22

The man in righteousness arrayed,
  A pure and blameless liver,
Needs not the keen Toledo blade,
  Nor venom-freighted quiver.

What though he wind his toilsome way
  O'er regions wild and weary—
Through Zara's burning desert stray,
  Or Asia's jungles dreary:

What though he plow the billowy deep
  By lunar light, or solar,
Meet the restless Simoom's sweep,
  Or iceberg circumpolar!
In bog or quagmire deep and dank
  His foot shall never settle;
He mounts the summit of Mont Blanc,
  Or Popocatapetl.

On Chimborazo's breathless height
  He treads o'er burning lava;
Or snuffs the Bohan Upas blight,
  The deathful plant of Java.
Through every peril he shall pass,
  By virtue's shield protected;
And still by Truth's unerring glass
  His path shall be directed.

Else wherefore was it, Thursday last,
  While strolling down the valley,
Defenseless, musing as I passed
  A canzonet to Sally,
A wolf, with mouth-protruding snout,
  Forth from the thicket bounded—
I clapped my hands and raised a shout—
  He heard—and fled—confounded.

Tangier nor Tunis never bred
  An animal more crabbèd;
Nor Fez, dry-nurse of lions, fed
  A monster half so rabid;
Nor Ararat so fierce a beast
  Has seen since days of Noah;
Nor stronger, eager for a feast,
  The fell constrictor boa.

                    translated by JOHN QUINCY ADAMS

OH SHIP! NEW BILLOWS SWEEP THEE OUT

Odes, I, 14

Oh Ship! new billows sweep thee out
Seaward. What wilt thou? Hold the port, be stout
    See'st not thy mast
How rent by stiff Southwestern blast?

Thy side, of rowers how forlorn?
Thine hull, with groaning yards, with rigging torn,
    Can ill sustain
The fierce, and ever fiercer main;

Thy gods, no more than sails entire,
From whom yet once thy need might aid require,
   Oh Pontic Pine,
The first of woodland stocks is thine,

Yet race and name are but as dust.
Not painted sterns give storm-tost seamen trust;
   Unless thou dare
To be the sport of storms, beware.

O fold at best a weary weight,
A yearning care and constant strain of late,
   O shun the seas
That gird those glittering Cyclades.

            translated by WILLIAM EWART GLADSTONE

BOY, I HATE THEIR EMPTY SHOWS

Odes, I, 38

Boy, I hate their empty shows,
   Persian garlands I detest,
Bring not me the late-blown rose
   Lingering after all the rest:

Plainer myrtle pleases me
   Thus outstretched beneath my vine,
Myrtle more becoming thee,
   Waiting with thy master's wine.

            translated by WILLIAM COWPER

NAY, XANTHIAS, FEEL UNASHAMED

Odes, II, 4

Nay, Xanthias, feel unashamed
   That she you love is but a servant.
Remember, lovers far more famed
   Were just as fervent.

Achilles loved the pretty slave
   Brisëis for her fair complexion;
And to Tecmessa Ajax gave
   His young affection.

Why, Agamemnon at the height
   Of feasting, triumph, and anointment,
Left everything to keep, one night,
   A small appointment.

And are you sure the girl you love—
   This maid on whom you have your heart set
Is lowly—that she is not of
   The Roman smart set?

A maiden modest as is she,
  So full of sweetness and forbearance,
Must be all right; her folks must be
  Delightful parents.

Her arms and face I can commend,
  And, as the writer of a poem,
I fain would compliment, old friend,
  The limbs below 'em.

Nay, be not jealous. Stop your fears.
  My tendencies are far from sporty.
Besides, the number of my years
  Is over forty.

  translated by FRANKLIN PIERCE ADAMS

RECEIVE, DEAR FRIEND, THE TRUTHS I TEACH

Odes, II, 10

Receive, dear friend, the truths I teach;
So shalt thou live beyond the reach
  Of adverse Fortune's power;
Not always tempt the distant deep,
Nor always timorously creep
  Along the treacherous shore.

He that holds fast the golden mean,
And lives contentedly between
  The little and the great,
Feels not the wants that pinch the poor,
Nor plagues that haunt the rich man's door,
  Embittering all his state.

The tallest pines feel most the power
Of wintry blasts; the loftiest tower
  Comes heaviest to the ground;
The bolts that spare the mountain's side,
His cloud-capped eminence divide,
  And spread the ruin round.

The well-informed philosopher
Rejoices with a wholesome fear,
  And hopes, in spite of pain;
If winter bellow from the north,
Soon the sweet spring comes dancing forth,
  And Nature laughs again.

What if thin heaven be overcast?
The dark appearance will not last;
  Expect a brighter sky.
The god, that strings the silver bow,
Awakes sometimes the Muses too,
  And lays his arrows by.

If hindrances obstruct thy way,
Thy magnanimity display,
    And let thy strength be seen;
But oh! if Fortune fill thy sail,
With more than a propitious gale,
    Take half thy canvas in.

               translated by WILLIAM COWPER

INVOCATION

Odes, I, 21

Maidens young and virgins tender,
Sing Diana in her splendor;
Boys at play within the hollow,
Sing the flowing-haired Apollo.

(Ye that, moved by love and duty,
Praise Diana's holy beauty,
Shall be granted joys unceasing
And, perhaps, a mate that's pleasing.)

(And if winning words we hit on,
Phœbus may present the Briton,
Persian, Parthian and the rest, with
All the wars and plagues *we're* blessed with.)

               translated by LOUIS UNTERMEYER

DESCENDED OF AN ANCIENT LINE

Odes, III, 29

Descended of an ancient line,
    That long the Tuscan scepter swayed,
Make haste to meet the generous wine,
    Whose piercing is for thee delayed:
    The rosy wreath is made;
And artful hands prepare
The fragrant Syrian oil, that shall perfume thy hair.

When the wine sparkles from afar,
    And the well-natured friend cries, come away;
Make haste and leave thy business and thy care,
    No mortal interest can be worth thy stay.
Leave, for a while, thy costly country seat;
And, to be great indeed, forget
The nauseous pleasures of the great.

    Make haste and come:
Come and forsake thy cloying store;
Thy turret that surveys from high
    The smoke, and wealth, and noise of Rome,
And all the busy pageantry
That wise men scorn, and fools adore.

Come, give thy soul a loose, and taste the pleasures of
    the poor.
Sometimes 'tis grateful for the rich to try
A short vicissitude, and fit of poverty:
  A savory dish, a homely treat,
  Where all is plain, where all is neat,
Without the stately spacious room,
The Persian carpet, or the Tyrian loom,
Clear up the cloudy foreheads of the great.

The sun is in the Lion mounted high;
  The Syrian star barks from afar,
And with his sultry breath infects the sky;
The ground below is parched, the heavens above us fry.
  The shepherd drives his fainting flock
  Beneath the covert of a rock,
And seeks refreshing rivulets nigh:
The sylvans to their shades retire,
Those very shades and streams new shades and streams
    require,
And want a cooling breeze of wind to fan the raging fire.
  Thou, what befits the new Lord Mayor;
  And what the city factions dare,
  And what the Gallic arms will do,
  And what the quiver-bearing foe,
Art anxiously inquisitive to know:
But God has wisely hid from human sight
  The dark decrees of future fate,
And sown their seeds in depths of night.
  He laughs at all the giddy turns of state,
  Where mortals search too soon, and fear too late.

Enjoy the present smiling hour,
And put it out of Fortune's power;
The tide of business like the running stream,
  Is sometimes high and sometimes low,
  A quiet ebb or a tempestuous flow,
And always in extreme.

Now with a noiseless gentle course
  It keeps within the middle bed;
  Anon it lifts aloft its head,
And bears down all before it with impetuous force;
  And trunks of trees come rolling down,
  Sheep and their folds together drown:
Both house and homestead into seas are borne,
And rocks are from their old foundations torn,
And woods, made thin with winds, their scattered honors
    mourn.

Happy the man, and happy he alone,
He, who can call to-day his own:
He who secure within, can say,
To-morrow do thy worst, for I have lived to-day.

Be fair or foul, or rain or shine,
The joys I have possessed, in spite of fate, are mine.
Not Heaven itself upon the past has power,
But what has been, has been, and I have had my hour.

Fortune that with malicious joy
    Does man, her slave, oppress,
Proud of her office to destroy,
    Is seldom pleased to bless:
Still various, and inconstant still,
But with an inclination to be ill,
Promotes, degrades, delights in strife,
And makes a lottery of life.
    I can enjoy her while she is kind;
    But when she dances in the wind,
And shakes her wings, and will not stay,
I puff the prostitute away;
    The little or the much she gave, is quietly resigned:
Content with poverty my soul I arm,
And Virtue, though in rags, will keep me warm.

                What is 't to me,
Who never sail in her unfaithful sea,
If storms arise, and clouds grow black;
If the mast split, and threaten wreck?
Then let the greedy merchant fear
    For his ill-gotten gain,
And pray to gods that will not hear
While the debating winds and billows bear
    His wealth unto the main.
For me, secure from Fortune's blows,
Secure of what I cannot lose,
In my small pinnace I can sail,
    Contemning all the blustering roar;
And running with a merry gale,
With friendly stars my safety seek
Within some little winding creek,
    And see the storm ashore.
                    translated by JOHN DRYDEN

VENUS, AGAIN THOU MOV'ST A WAR
Odes, IV, 1

Venus, again thou mov'st a war
    Long intermitted, pray thee, pray thee spare!
I am not such, as in the reign
    Of the good Cynara I was; refrain
Sour mother of sweet Loves, forbear
    To bend a man, now at his fiftieth year.

Too stubborn for commands so slack:
    Go where youth's soft entreaties call thee back.
More timely hie thee to the house

(With thy bright swans) of Paulus Maximus:
There jest and feast, make him thine host
  If a fit liver thou dost seek to toast.
For he's both noble, lovely, young,
  And for the troubled client fills his tongue:
Child of a hundred arts, and far
  Will he display the ensigns of thy war.

And when he, smiling, finds his grace
  With thee 'bove all his rivals' gifts take place,
He'll thee a marble statue make,
  Beneath a sweet-wood roof, near Alba lake;
There shall thy dainty nostril take
  In many a gum, and for thy soft ear's sake
Shall verse be set to harp and lute,
  And Phrygian hau'boy, not without the flute.
There twice a day in sacred lays,
  The youths and tender maids shall sing thy praise!
And in the Salian manner meet
  Thrice 'bout thy altar, with their ivory feet.

Me now, nor girl, nor wanton boy
  Delights, nor credulous hope of mutual joy;
Nor care I now healths to propound
  Or with fresh flowers to girt my temples round.
But why, or why, my Ligurine,
  Flow my thin tears down these pale cheeks of mine?
Or why my well-graced words among,
  With an uncomely silence, fails my tongue?
Hard-hearted, I dream every night
  I hold thee fast! but fled hence with the light,
Whether in Mars his field thou be,
  Or Tiber's winding streams, I follow thee.

                    translated by BEN JONSON

LEST YOU SHOULD THINK THAT VERSE
SHALL DIE

Odes, IV, 9

Lest you should think that verse shall die,
  Which sounds the silver Thames along,
Taught on the wings of truth to fly
  Above the reach of vulgar song;

Though daring Milton sits sublime,
  In Spenser native Muses play;
Nor yet shall Waller yield to time,
  Nor pensive Cowley's mortal lay.

Sages and chiefs long since had birth
  Ere Cæsar was, or Newton named;
These raised new empires o'er earth,
  And those, new heavens and systems framed.

Vain was the chief's, the sage's pride!
  They had no poet, and they died.
In vain they schemed, in vain they bled!
  They had no poet, and are dead.

translated by ALEXANDER POPE

OMIT, OMIT, MY SIMPLE FRIEND

Odes, II, 11

Omit, omit, my simple friend,
Still to inquire how parties tend,
Or what we fix with foreign powers.
If France and we are really friends,
And what the Russian Czar intends,
    Is no concern of ours.

Us not the daily quickening race
Of the invading populace
Shall draw to swell that shouldering herd.
Mourn will we not your closing hour,
Ye imbeciles in present power,
    Doomed, pompous, and absurd!

And let us bear, that they debate
Of all the engine-work of state,
Of commerce, laws, and policy,
The secrets of the world's machine,
And what the rights of man may mean,
    With readier tongue than we.

Only, that with no finer art
They cloak the troubles of the heart
With pleasant smile, let us take care;
Nor with a lighter hand dispose
Fresh garlands of this dewy rose,
    To crown Eugenia's hair.

Of little threads our life is spun,
And he spins ill, who misses one.
But is thy fair Eugenia cold?
Yet Helen had an equal grace,
And Juliet's was as fair a face,
    And now their years are told.

The day approaches, when we must
Be crumbling bones and windy dust;
And scorn us as our mistress may,
Her beauty will no better be
Than the poor face she slights in thee,
    When dawns that day, that day.

translated by MATTHEW ARNOLD